THE LAST
CHICAGO CUBS DYNASTY

THE LAST CHICAGO CUBS DYNASTY

Before the Curse

Hal Bock

ROWMAN & LITTLEFIELD
Lanham • Boulder • New York • London

Published by Rowman & Littlefield
A wholly owned subsidiary of The Rowman & Littlefield Publishing Group,
Inc.
4501 Forbes Boulevard, Suite 200, Lanham, Maryland 20706
www.rowman.com

Unit A, Whitacre Mews, 26-34 Stannary Street, London SE11 4AB

British Library Cataloguing in Publication Information Available

Library of Congress Cataloging-in-Publication Data

Names: Bock, Hal, author.
Title: The last Chicago Cubs dynasty : before the curse / Hal Bock.
Description: Lanham : ROWMAN & LITTLEFIELD, [2016] | Includes bibliographical refer-
   ences and index.
Identifiers: LCCN 2015035484| ISBN 9781442253308 (hardcover : alk. paper) | ISBN
   9781442253315 (ebook)
Subjects: LCSH: Chicago Cubs (Baseball team)—History—20th century. | Baseball players—
   United States—Biography.
Classification: LCC GV875.C6 B63 2016 | DDC 796.357/640977311—dc23
LC record available at http://lccn.loc.gov/2015035484

∞ ™ The paper used in this publication meets the minimum requirements of
American National Standard for Information Sciences Permanence of Paper
for Printed Library Materials, ANSI/NISO Z39.48-1992.

Printed in the United States of America

For the Bock Family Dynasty—my parents, who gave me the opportunity to follow my dream; son Richard, who makes me proud every day; daughter-in-law Caroline, a wonderful wife, mother, and magnificent author; Michael and Sara, world-class grandchildren; and, of course, my darling wife, Fran, who makes all things possible

CONTENTS

FOREWORD

Joe Mantegna

Actor Joe Mantegna of the TV show Criminal Minds *has been a Chicago Cubs fan all his life, accustomed to the peaks and valleys of rooting for this franchise. He helped create* Bleacher Bums, *a play that paid homage to the Wrigley Field faithful. In this foreword, he discusses the passion of Cubs Nation and the faithful fans who follow his team.*

There's a photograph of me at about nine years old, sitting in front of an old black-and-white television with a baseball mitt in my hand, watching Hank Sauer bat during a Cubs game at Wrigley Field (see the first photo in the photospread following chapter 5). It's the earliest visual evidence I have that I was an early victim of "The Curse." Now when I refer to that curse, I don't mean the one that goat owner supposedly cast on the Cubs when they refused entrance to his beloved pet. No, my curse is rooted in the amazement I still have knowing that millions of right-thinking people, myself included, have for generations now let ourselves be pained and punished by the outcome of an event that consists of grown men whacking a horsehide-covered ball with a wooden stick.

On the surface, it sounds like a tribal ceremony practiced by a prehistoric culture in some far off jungle. If only it was. My earliest memory of going to Cubs games was around five, when it became apparent to me that by growing up on the West Side of Chicago we had the opportunity to pick and choose our favorite team, as we weren't geographically locked into rooting for the Cubs or Sox based on North Side versus South. Sometimes I think the smelt in Lake Michigan are lucky to be the only thing on the East Side of Chicago, as they don't have to choose. For whatever reason, my dad was a Cubs fan. I never asked him how and why that happened, but it did. And therefore, I became one as well.

I do remember most of my friends in the neighborhood were Sox fans, and I especially remember 1959 when they had the opportunity to throw that in my face in light of the pennant win that year by the Pale Hose. I also remember distinctly being awoken by air-raid sirens as our dear Mayor Daley, Sox fan that he was, thought it was a good idea to celebrate that event by turning on the air-raid sirens and causing some people to jump into cars and head for Wisconsin. I remember my dad coming in my room and telling me not to worry; it was just a dumb way to celebrate the Sox victory. The look on my dad's face, as I think about it now, was that of someone who somehow knew he'd never live long enough to hear those sirens for *his* team. But we prevailed. Barely.

I remember when I was about seven years old, and my dad and I attended 10 games over that summer. And the Cubs lost every one. When he asked me to go to game 11, I politely declined. I actually began to believe my attendance was the cause of their losing, so I figured I'd make the ultimate sacrifice and help the team by not showing up. I should have gone. At about the age of 16 or so I became interested in becoming an actor, and one of the manifestations of that was that I would now look at the Cubs games I attended a little differently. As I knew the difficulty in getting people to attend theater, even when the reviews were good, I was astounded to witness the tens of thousands who would religiously attend the Cubs games to follow, at best, a mediocre team and continue to do so year after year with basically the same results. I then thought that if I could capture that fanaticism in a theatrical production I would have a hit on my hands. Thus the seeds of the play *Bleacher Bums*, which I conceived a few years later, were planted in my brain. While I always thought a play of this type would easily resonate with Cubs fans everywhere, I was pleasantly surprised to see that the play succeeded on a level much more far reaching than that. How else to explain its run in Los Angeles for 10 years straight and its continual run in theaters throughout the world since its inception in 1977. What it came down to is this: the Cubs became a metaphor for the underdog, the loser, loveable or not, that we as a species can't help but instinctively pull for. And it's that which tempers that earlier-mentioned Curse. As I've often said, it's easy being a Yankee fan; it takes real dedication, fortitude, and an endless supply of hope to follow our guys.

And it seems that hope does indeed spring eternal. It has for over the last 100 years anyway. Would I change anything? No. Because in my heart I actually believe that in following the Cubs we are perhaps holding the key to world peace. Crazy? Imagine this: The Cubs, at long last, prevail and win the world championship of baseball. And imagine further that the powers that be in baseball decide that this is now the perfect opportunity to abolish the sport, turn all the ballparks into soccer fields, and broadcast to the rest of the world that we've now made the ultimate sacrifice and have forsaken our national pastime to join the rest of the planet in their embrace of the "beautiful game." Think of it. Decades of fear and distrust of our country will dissolve overnight, and the Cubs will go down as the catalyst that ultimately secured peace and love throughout the world. I mean, why play on? What more do we have to prove? Still sound crazy? Probably. But really, is it any crazier than enduring a century of pain over guys whacking horsehide balls with wooden sticks?

ACKNOWLEDGMENTS

This book would not have been possible without the support of many people. First and most importantly, my wonderful wife, Fran, who rescued me countless times from computer malfunction when modern technology threatened to transport me back to a good, old-fashioned manual typewriter. I would be nowhere without her.

Then, the great actor Joe Mantegna, star of *Criminal Minds*, a Tony and Emmy winner and longtime fan, who agreed to write a thoughtful foreword about the passion Cubs fans share throughout the peaks and valleys experienced by their favorite team.

Then, those who sadly are gone. I was lucky enough to come along at a time when I could meet and chat, over 40 years of sportswriting, with many old-timers familiar with the lore and legend of the Cubs: people like Ernie Banks, Phil Cavarretta, and Charlie Grimm, who all played for the team in different eras, and Jerome Holtzman, Bill Gleason, James T. Farrell, and John Carmichael, a hall of fame of Chicago journalism, who were gracious with their time and shared many stories with me.

I was fortunate, too, for the wonderful books that have come before, particularly *Baseball: The Biographical Encyclopedia* and the Society for American Baseball Research publications, including *Deadball Stars of the National League*, which provided plentiful insight and anecdotes. Also, the Baseball Almanac website was a treasure trove of information. The same goes for the Society for American Baseball Research website. I also learned that the Library of Congress is one of the few places you can find photos from more than a century ago.

I am sincerely grateful to all of them.

CAST OF CHARACTERS

First Base

Frank Chance, 1898–1912; manager, 1905–1912. Managed Cubs to a record 116 wins in 1906 and career-winning percentage of .664 in seven and a half seasons. Nicknamed the "Peerless Leader" with four pennants and two World Series championships to his credit. Hit over .300 four times and led National League in stolen bases twice. Career batting average: .296.

Second Base

Johnny Evers, 1902–1913. Managed Cubs in 1913. Pivotal player in the Fred Merkle boner play when he called for the ball and claimed a force-out, negating an apparent winning run for the Giants and forcing a playoff game that led the Cubs to their last world championship in 1908. Played for Miracle Braves in 1914. Career batting average: .279.

Shortstop

Joe Tinker, 1902–1912. Managed Cubs in 1916. First link in the Tinker-to-Evers-to-Chance double-play unit during the Last

Chicago Cubs Dynasty. Finished career as player-manager for Cincinnati Reds, Chicago Feds, and the Cubs. Career batting average: .282.

Third Base

Harry Steinfeldt, 1906–1910. Answer to the eternal trivia question, who was the third baseman with Tinker, Evers, and Chance? Traded to the Cubs in 1906, led league with 176 hits and 83 RBIs while batting .327. Led all players with .471 batting average in 1907 World Series. Career batting average: .267.

Left Field

Jimmy Sheckard, 1906–1912. Was a left-handed slugger with Brooklyn before being traded to Chicago in 1905. Led National League in most offensive categories at one time or another including nine home runs in 1903 and 147 walks in 1911. Terrific defensive player in an era before Gold Gloves were awarded. Career batting average: .274.

Center Field

Jimmy Slagle, 1899–1908. Starred in the 1907 World Series when he led Cubs with four RBIs and six stolen bases including the first straight steal of home in a World Series game. Also scored the winning run in the series-winning fifth game. Career batting average: .268.

Right Field

Frank "Wildfire" Schulte, 1904–1916. A long ball threat at time when home runs were scarce. Had 92 career home runs, a high total for the Deadball Era. Stole home 22 times. Had a number of eccentricities including collecting hairpins, which he believed were a predictor of his hits. Nicknamed Wildfire because of his affection for actress Lillian Russell, who starred in a play of that name. Career batting average: .270.

Catcher

Johnny Kling, 1900–1911. Best defensive catcher of baseball's Deadball Era. From 1902 to 1908, led National League catchers in putouts six times, fielding percentage twice and assists and double plays once. Champion pocket billiards player. Left baseball to defend title in 1909 but was unsuccessful before returning to Cubs in 1910. Career batting average: .272.

Right-Handed Pitcher

Mordecai "Three Finger" Brown, 1904–1912, 1916. Right hand was mangled in farm accident when he was seven, leading to nickname. Pitches had strange spin that baffled batters. Traded to Cubs by St. Louis in 1904. Posted 26–6 record in 1906 with 1.04 earned run average (ERA), lowest for any pitcher in 20th century and third lowest in Major League history. W–L: 239–130, ERA: 2.06.

Ed Reulbach, 1905–1913. Pitched shutouts in both ends of a doubleheader against Brooklyn. Threw two one-hitters, six two-hitters, and thirteen three-hitters in his career. Threw a one-hitter in 1908 World Series against the Tigers. Had winning streaks of 17 games and 14 games; only 20th century pitcher with two streaks of 14 wins. W–L: 182–106, ERA: 2.28.

Orval Overall, 1906–1910, 1913. Curve ball specialist whose 2.23 earned run average was ninth best in Major League history for pitchers with 1,500 innings. Cubs Opening Day pitcher every year from 1906 to 1910. Was 3–1 with 1.75 ERA in four World Series. W–L: 108–71, ERA: 2.23.

Left-Handed Pitcher

Jack Pfiester, 1906–1911. Cubs' Giant killer, compiled 15–5 record against Chicago's hated rivals. Specialized in a sidearm delivery and possessed one of the best pickoff moves of the Deadball Era. Lifetime 2.02 ERA was third best all-time for pitchers with 1,000 innings. W–L: 71–44, ERA: 2.02.

Bench

Solly Hofman, 1904–1912, 1916. Nicknamed "Circus Solly" after comic strip character of the time. He claimed it was for his circus catches in center field. Played every position except pitcher and catcher and was considered the game's best utility man before taking over center field in 1909. Relayed Al Bridwell's hit to Johnny Evers, touching off the Fred Merkle baserunning blunder episode in 1908. Career batting average: .269.

Heinie Zimmerman, 1907–1926. Combative character who was involved in numerous brawls with opponents and teammates. Versatile player capable of playing second, third, and shortstop. Led National League with .372 batting average and 14 home runs in 1912. Missed Triple Crown by three RBIs. Career batting average: .295.

CHRONOLOGY

1903

As baseball weaved its way into American consciousness, there were many excesses in the game. On May 6, the Chicago White Sox committed 12 errors in one game against Detroit. On June 2, the Pittsburgh Pirates won a tripleheader from the Brooklyn Dodgers. On June 25, Boston's Wiley Piatt became the first 20th-century pitcher to lose two complete games in one day, beaten 1–0 and 5–3 by Pittsburgh.

Joe McGinnity of the New York Giants won three doubleheaders in the month of August, beating Boston 4–1 and 5–2 on August 1, defeating Brooklyn 6–1 and 4–3 a week later, and then completing his personal trifecta by beating Philadelphia 4–1 and 9–2 on August 31. He threw 434 innings that season, an unheard-of workload in modern baseball with its pitch count and innings count restrictions on pitchers.

Not all pitchers were as efficient as McGinnity. On August 26, the Philadelphia Phillies walked 17 Brooklyn batters in a single game.

In the days after Boston and Pittsburgh played the first World Series, brothers Wilbur and Orville Wright continued to tinker with a machine that would redefine travel in the 20th

century. Four test flights on December 17 introduced the
concept of manned flight.

1904

St. Louis hosted a World's Fair where, among other things, the
ice cream cone was introduced as a frozen delicacy that
would delight generations to come. An estimated 20 million
people visited the fair, dressed in Sunday finery, women in
flowered hats, men in derbies and straw skimmers, to see
demonstrations of art, science, and industry. The city also
played host that summer to the Olympic Games, conducted
on a much smaller scale than the event would grow into
later in the century.

That summer in baseball, a young Georgian broke in, destined
to become one of the game's most compelling stars. Ty
Cobb was just another rookie when he showed up with Au-
gusta of the South Atlantic League on April 21. Of more
interest was the remarkable 41-win season put together by
Jack Chesbro of the Highlanders, who were not yet the
Yankees. Chesbro had a streak of 30 complete games that
season.

Cy Young of Boston pitched a perfect game against Philadelphia on May 5, and teammate Jesse Tannehill threw a no-
hitter against the White Sox on August 17. On June 11, Bob
Wicker of the Cubs held the Giants hitless into the 10th
inning before winning 1–0 in 12 innings on a one-hitter.

Perhaps the most significant baseball event of the summer
from the Cubs standpoint, however, occurred on May 30
when Frank Chance was hit by pitches five times in a doubleheader. It was not an unusual circumstance for Chance,
the first baseman and manager of the Last Chicago Cubs
Dynasty to be targeted by pitchers. He lost the hearing in

one ear and developed a blood clot on the brain due to his frequent beanings. The injuries led to his early retirement from the game.

The New York Giants won 18 straight games from June 6 through July 4 on the way to a National League pennant but not the World Series when manager John McGraw decided to snub the insurgents from the American League.

1905

Ty Cobb made his Major League debut in the summer of 1905 with the Detroit Tigers. It came just weeks after Cobb's mother, mistaking her husband for an intruder, shot and killed his father. The episode was often cited as the reason Cobb became such a violent player in an otherwise nonviolent sport.

Another player made his debut that summer. Outfielder Archibald "Moonlight" Graham broke in with the Giants against the Brooklyn Superbas on June 29, sent out to play right field. He was on deck in the ninth inning when Claude Elliot made the last out. Graham returned to right field for the bottom of the ninth of the 11–1 Giants victory. It turned out to be the only Major League game of his career. He became well known though as a central character in *Shoeless Joe*, an iconic baseball novel by W. P. Kinsella, and the subsequent 1989 motion picture *Field of Dreams*.

Alarmed by the number of injuries in football, President Theodore Roosevelt summoned 60 colleges to Washington on October 9, 1905, to discuss the issue. The result was the introduction of the forward pass as an offensive alternative to the collisions that led to the deaths of 18 players and 159 serious injuries in 1905.

When the New York Giants returned to the World Series in 1905, Christy Mathewson produced the greatest display of pitching in the history of the event, throwing complete game shutouts against Philadelphia in Game One, Game Three, and Game Five, 27 scoreless innings over a stretch of six days. Mathewson's remarkable achievement made the Giants World Series champions.

1906

On April 18, the tranquility of a California morning was destroyed by a devastating earthquake. San Francisco was set on fire by ruptured gas mains. Eighty percent of the city was gone. The economic loss was estimated at $400 million. Three thousand people died and three hundred thousand were left homeless by a disaster of monumental proportions.

When Connie Mack found himself short of outfielders on May 8, he sent pitcher Chief Bender into the game in the sixth inning. Bender responded by hitting two inside-the-park home runs.

The Cubs swept an Independence Day doubleheader from the Pirates, winning both games 1–0. In the opener, "Three Finger" Brown and Lefty Leifield both pitched one-hitters with Leifield getting the lone Pirates hit.

On August 3, Long Tom Hughes of the Washington Senators and Fred Glade of the St. Louis Browns were locked in a scoreless tie after nine innings. Hughes homered to win the game in the 10th, the first pitcher to pitch a shutout and account for the game's only run with a home run.

The Chicago White Sox beat the Chicago Cubs in six games despite batting just .198 and committing 15 errors in what is considered the greatest World Series upset in history.

1907

A major financial catastrophe was averted when a group of Wall Street businessmen headed by J. P. Morgan pledged $25 million to invest in shares of the plunging New York Stock Exchange, ending the bank panic of 1907 and leading to the establishment of the Federal Reserve System.

On June 28, with Branch Rickey catching for the New York Highlanders, the Washington Nationals stole 13 bases. Rickey did not catch another game that season.

Walter Johnson made his debut for Washington on August 2, 1907, against Detroit. The first hit he allowed was a bunt single by Ty Cobb.

Hall of Fame catcher Roger Bresnahan of the New York Giants wore the first standard pair of shin guards on April 11, 1907, in a game against the Philadelphia Phillies.

The Chicago Cubs, still stung by their stunning World Series loss to the Chicago White Sox a year earlier, swept the Detroit Tigers to win the Series.

1908

A two-year investigation by the Mills Commission determined that Civil War general Abner Doubleday invented baseball in Cooperstown, New York. That theory was later discarded, and Alexander Cartwright, who came up with the first set of rules, is now credited with the game's development.

Honus Wagner announced his retirement from the Pittsburgh Pirates at age 34 in March and then changed his mind and went on to win his sixth batting title and lead the league in hits, total bases, doubles, triples, runs batted in, and stolen bases.

The Detroit Tigers turned triple plays on consecutive days
June 6–7 against the Boston Red Sox.

Celebrated outlaws Butch Cassidy and the Sundance Kid were
reported surrounded and killed by soldiers in Bolivia on
November 6, although there were rumors that both escaped
and their grave sites are unmarked.

1909

Construction began on the ocean liner *Titanic*. The project
would take three years, and the glamorous vessel sank on its
first voyage, April 10, 1912.

Honus Wagner stole his way around the bases on May 2 and
then duplicated the feat the next day, the third and fourth
times he did that in his career.

The Chicago White Sox set a modern Major League record by
stealing 12 bases including three of home in a 15–3 rout of
the St. Louis Browns on July 2.

Ty Cobb led the American League with nine home runs, all of
them inside the park, the only player in history to lead the
league in homers without hitting one out of the park.

1910

President William Howard Taft began a presidential tradition
by throwing out the first pitch of the baseball season at
Washington. Walter Johnson marked the occasion with a
one-hitter.

Chief Bender pitched a no-hitter on May 10 for the Philadelphia against Cleveland. He missed a perfect game when he
walked Terry Turner, who was thrown out trying to steal
second base.

On July 4, African American heavyweight champion Jack Johnson defended his title against James J. Jeffries, who came
out of retirement and lost 100 pounds to take the fight.
Jeffries was the latest "Great White Hope" to face Johnson,
who won a one-sided fight in 15 rounds. Race riots followed
the fight, and 20 people died.

Cy Young won his 500th game on July 19, pitching Cleveland
past Washington 5–4. The winningest pitcher in Major
League history finished his career with 511 victories.

I

PRELUDE TO A DYNASTY

Before the 20th century, when horse-drawn carriages and handlebar mustaches dotted America's landscape, baseball was not yet the country's national pastime. It was, in fact, far removed from that status, viewed as little more than an afterthought by a nation rubbing the sleep out of its eyes as it prepared for life in a new century and all the excitement that prospect brought with it.

Just ahead were marvelous changes forged by Henry Ford's remarkable new motorized automobile and the Wright brothers' experiments with a flying machine. Baseball was hardly mainstream, largely ignored by a country with other things on its mind. It was widely viewed as a game played by transients and miscreants, the underbelly of society—hardly worth any serious attention. And some of the players of that era did nothing to repair that image. They were viewed as a ragtag bunch of hard-drinking malingerers who could not hold a real job in a land that was just beginning to throw off the shackles of post–Civil War America, moving into the expansion and opportunity of a new century.

In Chicago, there was an attempt to build a powerhouse team that would command attention, a team like the one the city enjoyed two decades before when it won five pennants in seven years under the leadership of Cap Anson. With Anson gone, the team had struggled and eventually imported a slight, balding man with one of those handsome handlebar moustaches to reconstruct the franchise. Frank Selee had managed the Boston Beaneaters—who would later become the Braves—to five pennants in 12 seasons including baseball's first 100-win season in 1898 before the core of his team was lured away from Boston by the rival American League. When the team fell apart, Selee was fired, but he wasn't out of work very long. Chicago owner Jim Hart quickly hired him to rebuild his team.

Chicago deserved a dominant team. After all, it was a cornerstone franchise in baseball, created in 1876 as an original member of the new National League. At the time, the team was called the White Stockings and was manned with players lured from other teams by William Hulbert, who owned a Chicago team in the old National Association, where gambling, drunkenness, and other socially unacceptable behaviors were the norm. Hulbert was disgusted by the atmosphere. It was unbecoming of his hometown.

Proud of its role as host to the Republican Party Convention in 1860, where Abraham Lincoln had been nominated for president, Chicago—the country's second largest city—was emerging as the hub of a new America. Its economy and population flourished during the Civil War. Railroads ran through the city. Manufacturing became a mainstay. It was, as Frank Sinatra would note a century or so later, "a toddlin' town."

And then it burned down.

Six years after the end of the Civil War, much of the city was destroyed by the Great Chicago Fire, believed to have been started when Mrs. O'Leary's legendary cow kicked over a lantern. That story may have been pure fiction, and the cow may have been an innocent bystander. But the fact of the matter is Chicago, a city with panache, was reduced to rubble by a blaze that raged for two days, October 9–10, 1871. The fire killed 300 people, left

100,000 homeless, and destroyed 18,000 buildings. The city was devastated.

After the blaze, Joseph Medill, publisher of the *Chicago Tribune*, ran for mayor with the platform "Fireproof." He won the office, one of the first of a series of strange election-day choices by the city's population. Consider that some years later, Mayor Carter H. Harrison captured the fancy of his town by riding around on a white horse, waving his hat to onlookers.

Among the fire's casualties was Lake Front Park, a converted dumping ground located on the shores of Lake Michigan, where the local baseball team played. After the fire, the White Stockings rebuilt and moved into the 23rd Street grounds, but three years later another fire swept through downtown Chicago. This one forced the visiting Philadelphia Athletics to flee to another hotel, left some White Stockings players homeless, and limited attendance for that day's game to only 500 or 600 fans, far short of the expected 5,000 to 6,000. The team moved on to two more parks before settling in West Side Park, where another fire interrupted a game on August 5, 1894. Two players, Jimmy Ryan and Walt Wilmot, used bats to break through a barbed-wire fence and rescue 1,600 fans, leading them on to the playing field. The team drifted through two more parks before finding a permanent home in Wrigley Field, where ivy, planted by Bill Veeck, now decorates the outfield walls.

The one constant in the old National Association was the astounding success of the Boston Red Stockings, who won four straight championships. That state of affairs stuck in William Hulbert's craw. Angered by Boston's dominance, Hulbert struck back, using lucrative contracts to lure their best players to his team in Chicago and getting them to trade in their Red Stockings for white ones, changing the balance of power in the league. And if Hulbert's partners in the National Association didn't like that, well, he had a solution for that problem, too. He simply created a whole new league for himself and his team, one that would demand better behavior from the players.

The entry fee for joining the new National League was the princely sum of $100, and teams from St. Louis, Hartford, New York, Louisville, Philadelphia, Cincinnati, and Boston signed on to join Chicago, each equipped with Hulbert's requirement that it have a population of at least 75,000. Teams would play a 70-game schedule, and the league champions would be awarded a pennant costing at least $100, matching its original fee for joining the league. Umpires were paid $5 per game.

Hulbert's goal was to establish his league as a viable enterprise. Baseball was a vastly different game as the new league took shape. Pitchers threw underhand from 45 feet, not 60 feet, 6 inches. Batters could request pitches in a specific location—high, low, inside, and outside. Fielders wore no conventional gloves. The biggest difference between Hulbert's new National League and the old National Association involved the behavior of the players. Hulbert preached clean play: no drinking, gambling, or rowdiness in his new league. This was no simple matter with the roustabouts who played the game in those days.

Typical of the take-no-prisoners style of play of that time was Honus Wagner's experience in his second Major League at-bat, playing for Louisville against John McGraw's Baltimore Orioles. Wagner hit a ball into the outfield gap, a sure triple. But he never reached third base, first encountering a textbook hip check by first baseman Jack Doyle and then a roadblock at second base from Hugh Jennings. When he finally reached third base, McGraw had the ball waiting and shoved a hard tag into the rookie's midsection that left Wagner gasping for air.

Message sent. Message received.

In his next time around the bases, Wagner bowled over Doyle and Jennings and crashed into McGraw. The rookie went on to bat .344 that season, the first of 17 consecutive .300 seasons, eight of them as the National League batting champion.

Well aware of the game's ruffian reputation, Hulbert was serious about imposing better behavior standards. When he was presented with evidence that four Louisville players had fixed games, he didn't hesitate to act decisively. The most significant player involved was pitcher Jim Devlin, who mysteriously lost his effectiveness during a late-season swoon that cost Louisville the league title. When club president Charles E. Chase confronted Devlin, one of the other conspirators, George Hall, thought the pitcher had confessed and admitted his role in the plot. When it was over, Devlin, Hall, infielder Albert Nichols, and team captain Bill Craver were thrown out of the league, and the team folded. It was baseball's first gambling scandal. Sadly, it would not be the last.

Louisville wasn't the only team to disappear. New York and Philadelphia dropped out after failing to make their last road trips in that first season. Milwaukee and Indianapolis arrived for brief stays and left just as quickly. Finances were a constant problem for the league. Teams were added and dropped at a dizzying pace. The one constant, however, was Hulbert's franchise. Chicago was in the league to stay and on its way to becoming the oldest continuous franchise in Major League baseball.

The city recovered quickly from the Great Fire of 1871. Much of the debris was dumped into Lake Michigan as landfill, creating the foundations of two parks and the Art Institute of Chicago. Twenty-two years after the fire, the city hosted the Columbian Exposition, a sort of World's Fair that celebrated the renaissance of Chicago. The affair headlined the exotic dancer Little Egypt and featured the first and largest Ferris wheel of its time.

Hulbert did his part in the reconstruction of his city, introducing his new baseball league and planting the seeds for his team to dominate it.

When he stocked his new team, Hulbert's biggest coup was to lure pitcher Albert Spalding away from the Red Stockings. Or did Spalding lure Hulbert? There are conflicting versions of how these two men came together, but their liaison would be a defining moment in the history of Chicago baseball, especially since Spalding brought three other teammates along for the ride. Hulbert's overture to Spalding involved geography. The pitcher had his roots in Illinois before migrating to Boston. When Hulbert approached him, he told Spalding the pitcher had no business in the East. "You're a Western boy," he said. "You belong right here (in Chicago)."[1]

That argument made enough sense to Spalding that he convinced three teammates to join the exodus from Boston to Chicago, bringing along first baseman Cal McVey, second baseman Ross Barnes, and catcher Deacon White. Opening Day was April 25, 1876, and Spalding delivered an immediate dividend, pitching a 4–0 shutout at Louisville. He also had the first hit in Cubs history. A week later, Barnes hit the first home run in National League history in a 15–9 victory at Cincinnati. The inside-the-park home run was his only one all year. Hulbert's team was off and running.

In their first year in Chicago, Barnes won the batting title with a .404 average, White led the league with 60 runs batted in, and McVey batted .345. On consecutive days in July, McVey had a pair of six-hit games, a feat that has never been duplicated. Hulbert was a happy man. And Spalding had a lot to do with the owner's condition.

That was a temporary situation, though. In their second year, Spalding could no longer pitch and moved to first base. Without a reserve clause to restrict him, White made a U-turn and returned to Boston. Barnes missed more than half the season because of injury, and Chicago tumbled to fifth place.

White, a 2013 inductee to the Hall of Fame, played for Cleveland when the National Association was created in 1871. He is credited with the first Major League hit on May 4 against Fort Wayne and the first extra base hit, a double. He was also an innovator, introducing a catcher's mitt and mask to the challenging job behind the plate. "In those days, the catcher stood far behind the batter," White said years later. "He caught the ball on the first bounce. I got the idea of using a glove, made a mask for my face and stood right behind the batter. That caused a sensation."[2]

Paying attention was White's buddy, Al Spalding, who liked the idea of the mask so much that it became one of the first products he produced when he moved into the sporting goods business after his baseball career was over.

The pitcher, whose motto was "everything is possible to him who dares,"[3] had won 204 games in the National Association and did not come to Chicago cheaply, commanding a $2,000 salary, 25 percent of the gate, and the dual role of pitcher-manager. To sweeten the pot, Hulbert turned over operation of the team's business affairs to Spalding, put him on the team's board of directors, and gave him a stake in the team's ownership as well. Eventually, Spalding would become president and then owner of the Chicago franchise.

Spalding was an entrepreneur, always looking for the next big thing. While occupied with pitching for Chicago, he also gained the rights to publish an annual baseball guide. For a cover price of 10 cents, the guide provided readers with rosters of all National League teams as well as the rules of the game and included an autographed portrait of the pitcher. The back of the guide featured advertisements for equipment, everything from a "featherweight" baseball shoe to official league balls, uniforms, and even fencing equipment, all of it conveniently available from A. G. Spalding & Brothers, the pitcher's sporting goods company, a sideline that became one of the biggest athletic supplies businesses in the country.

Spalding was also a rather good judge of baseball talent. After signing with Chicago, he quickly advised Hulbert that while he was at the business of importing players for his team, he might want to look into Philadelphia's first baseman-catcher, a fellow named Adrian "Cap" Anson.

That turned out to be a pretty good tip. Anson was a professional hitter, one of the National Association's best players. He batted over .300 in 24 of his 27 Major League seasons and was the first player to accumulate 3,000 hits in his career. He was a large man and a commanding presence on the field. He liked to bait umpires and opponents, and if he was a bit rough-edged for the quaint rules of the new National League, Hulbert looked the other way and signed him up.

But Anson almost never made it to the new city and new league. There was a complication because his girlfriend, Virginia Fiegal, had no interest in relocating from Philadelphia to Chicago. So after signing with Hulbert, Anson had a change of heart over this affair of the heart and twice tried to buy his way out of his contract, offering $1,000 for his release. Hulbert was having none of that, and Spalding helped sweet-talk Anson back to the new team where he would wind up staying for 22 years.

Spalding and the other Boston expatriates took Chicago to the pennant in 1876, the National League's first season, a singular accomplishment. In addition to managing the team, the pitcher won 47 games with a 1.75 earned run average (ERA) and batted .312 as a part-time first baseman–outfielder. He should have taken better care of his arm though. Worn out by the workload, he won just one game the next season and soon was off to concentrate on his successful sporting goods company. And he also cashed in on the other parts of Hulbert's bargain, becoming the boss of the ball club. In 1879, with Spalding off to follow other pursuits including the lucrative manufacture of bats, gloves, balls, and uniforms, Anson became the team's manager, a job he would keep until 1897.

In 1880, one year after Anson took over as manager, the White Stockings won three straight pennants. They won 21 consecutive games that year from June 2 through July 8. The centerpiece of their pitching staff was Larry Corcoran, the only pitcher in team history to throw three no-hitters. Corcoran turned the trick in 1880, when he won 43 games, and in 1882 and from then through he won 170 games. He also became famous for being the first pitcher to communicate with his catcher from the mound. He would chew a huge wad of tobacco, and when he shifted it from one side of his mouth to the other, it tipped off catcher Silver Flint as to what pitch Corcoran would throw.

Corcoran also hit the first grand-slam home run in team history, connecting against Worcester's Lee Richmond on June 20, 1882. It was one of only two homers he hit in his eight-year career.

Hulbert was still in the business of bringing the best players he could to Chicago. So when Anson mentioned Cincinnati's strapping young outfielder Mike "King" Kelly, the owner gave his manager the green light to sign him. Kelly, the son of a Civil War soldier, had can't-miss credentials after batting .348 in 1879. Hulbert made the acquisition a bit simpler by dismissing the Cincinnati team from the National League for selling liquor on the ball club's grounds.

Truth be known, Kelly enjoyed a sip or two of the bubbly now and then too. Now a free agent, he was approached by Anson. The negotiations were not simple. Kelly wanted $100 more than Anson was offering. The talks dragged on for weeks before Anson capitulated. Kelly would get the extra $100 and become a central character in the success of his new team.

A hundred dollars was no small piece of change as far as Anson was concerned. In his autobiography, Connie Mack recalled that in 1883, he and some teammates on a local team in East Brookfield, Massachusetts, made a bold proposal to Anson. If he would consider a stop off for his Chicago team on their way back from Boston, why, the citizenry of East Brookfield would gladly guarantee the team $100 for its trouble.

No problem. Anson accepted, and the East Brookfield boys hurriedly cleaned up the local field, which was littered with debris. Anson's team came to town, and the locals passed the hat, collecting just enough change to cover the guarantee. Anson's team, King Kelly included, played the game, took the $100, and went on its way.

Anson was not always so agreeable. In 1883, at an exhibition game in Toledo, Ohio, he was outraged at the presence of an African American player, Moses Fleetwood Walker, on the other team. He threatened to pull his team off the field but relented when it was suggested that if he did that, his team would not get paid. So Walker played and so did the White Stockings. On another occasion, he pulled his team off the field in Newark, refusing to play because pitcher George Storey, another African American, was on the other team. The episodes of racism put a stain on Anson's reputation and began a whites-only trend in organized baseball that did not end until Jackie Robinson signed with the Brooklyn Dodgers' Montreal farm team in 1945.

Kelly was the swashbuckling poster boy of a rollicking era in baseball, a fan favorite for his elegantly styled moustache and raucous approach to the game. Typical of that was his baserunning style. He perfected the hook slide to avoid tags, thought nothing of kicking the ball out of a fielder's glove, and stole bases long before it became a widely used strategy. His daring on the base paths led to the popular fans' chant of "slide, Kelly, slide!"

But Kelly's affection for liquid refreshment inevitably led to trouble, and Spalding, by then in charge of the White Stockings, decided he could no longer endure his star's nocturnal adventures. After the 1886 season—the last of Anson's string of pennants and a year in which Kelly batted .388—Spalding dispatched his star slugger to Boston, sold for the unheard-of fee of $10,000. Kelly, equipped with two batting championships, agreed to the deal, provided he was guaranteed $4,000. He was welcomed in Boston like royalty, treated like a conquering hero, given a place to live, and brought to and from games in a carriage pulled by a pair of white horses.

Kelly was liberal with baseball advice, friendly tips from a superstar to those just starting out in the game. "When you go to bat, swing the bat gently," he advised in his autobiography. "If the ball is coming quick, it won't require a great amount of strength to send it far. Then run for your life, and don't be afraid to slide." It seemed obvious advice from the man whom fans always reminded to "slide, Kelly, slide!"

Anson managed Chicago to five pennants in seven seasons from 1880 to 1886, Major League baseball's first dynasty. Typical was a game in 1883 when the White Stockings scored 18 runs on 18 hits in the seventh inning of a 25–6 victory over Detroit. Anson is also credited with incorporating some of the game's greatest innovations including the hit-and-run, platoons, pitching rotations, and the value of spring training. His reign was not serene though. He drove his players hard, conducting daily workouts that were demanding and bed checks that were understandably unpopular with players who enjoyed a bit of nightlife. And when the team didn't perform up to his high standards, Anson railed at the players, calling them "a bunch of drunkards and loafers." He was a self-proclaimed tough guy and admitted as much in his autobiography, candidly writing, "I was a natural-born kicker, bent upon making trouble for others. The scrapes I managed to get into were too numerous to mention."

He also was something of a showman. He liked to celebrate Chicago championships by parading his players from their hotel to road ballparks in open carriages, hoping to antagonize local citizens who might then buy tickets to the game to razz his players. And there were championships to celebrate, three in a row from 1880 to 1882 and two more in 1885 and 1886.

Anson became the team's manager in 1879, and the White Stockings' roster was strengthened when the Milwaukee and Indianapolis franchises folded and Chicago inherited outfielder Abner Dalrymple, catcher Silver Flint, and third baseman Ned Williamson. The team struggled in his first season, a painful year for Anson who was sidelined by a kidney infection. A year later, however, Anson's juggernaut took off.

Chicago won the pennant by 15 games in 1880, compiling a record of 67–17, a record .798 winning percentage that no team has ever approached again. The stars were Dalrymple, who led the league in hits (126) and runs scored (91); center fielder George Gore, the batting champion with a .360 average; and pitchers Corcoran, whose 43 wins came with a 1.95 earned run average, and Fred Goldsmith, who went 21–3.

Anson's team repeated as champions in 1881 and 1882, and after also-ran seasons in 1883 and 1884, Chicago returned to the top for two more titles, giving Anson's boys five championships in seven years. Meanwhile, Albert Spalding flexed his muscles with the league, forcing a change in the Lake Front Park ground rules. The cozy venue had fences that were 196 feet away in left field and 180 feet in right. Balls hit over those close-in fences had been doubles, but under Spalding's urging they became home runs. Suddenly, the White Stockings became a team of sluggers, hitting 142 home runs, all but 10 of them at home. Williamson led the barrage with a league-leading 27, including three in one game.

Anson had 21, including five in two days, and second baseman Fred Pfeffer had 25. The production was in stark contrast to the 1877 season when the White Stockings became the only National League team to go through a season without hitting any home runs.

A year after the home run barrage, when the team moved to the original West Side Park, the home run total dwindled to 54, but the White Stockings won another pennant anyway, prevailing in a season-long race with the New York Giants, a hint of a rivalry to come after the turn of the century.

Anson's hard-edged approach did not exactly endear him to his players, and tension prevailed. There was a wholesale exodus of his team in 1889 when the new Players League lured most of his roster away. Anson stayed, and the team survived. But soon, hard times set in for the franchise, and by 1902, Frank Selee was imported to oversee the team's reconstruction.

A soft-spoken man who never played a game in the Major Leagues, Selee was a welcome change for the Cubs players who had endured Anson's roughshod style. "If I make things pleasant for the players they reciprocate," Selee once noted. "I want them to be temperate and live properly. I do not believe that men who are engaged in such exhilarating exercise should be kept in strait jackets all the time, but I expect them to be in condition to play. I do not want a man who cannot appreciate such treatment."[4]

Taking over a team that was a woeful 53–86 in 1901, Selee faced a daunting task. A shrewd evaluator of baseball talent, the onetime watchmaker and haberdasher started mixing and matching the Cubs players. Piece by piece, he assembled a team that would compete for the league lead.[5]

With the World Series starting in 1903, the proprietors of other franchises decided to arrange intracity series. By then, Chicago had a second team, and the new White Sox provided an instant rivalry that created a 15-game showdown—the first Chicago City

Series, which proved to be a turning point for the Cubs make-over.

Even though he pitched a three-hit shutout and won the first game 11–0, there were rumors that pitcher Jack Taylor had conspired with gamblers to fix three other games that he lost 10–3, 9–2, and 4–2. Although Taylor denied the charges, the National Commission, which ruled baseball at the time, investigated and fined him. Despite his slight size—he was only 5 foot 10 and 170 pounds—Taylor was a workhorse. He had a stretch of 187 consecutive complete games including one that went 19 innings and another that stretched 18. He pitched both games of a doubleheader and, in six of his ten seasons, pitched more than 300 innings. But when suspicions rose around him, he was quickly shipped out of Chicago in a four-player trade with the St. Louis Cardinals that delivered another pitcher. Mordecai "Three Finger" Brown would become one of baseball's most dominant pitchers.

Brown had a mediocre start with the Cardinals, going 9–13 in his rookie season. But after the trade, he would never be mediocre again, winding up with 239 wins in a Hall of Fame career with the Cubs.

Selee was assembling a strong team, but he would not live to see the fruits of his efforts. A hacking cough was soon diagnosed as tuberculosis, and he was forced to retire during the 1905 season, replaced by first baseman Frank Chance, who had reluctantly switched from catcher. Four years later, Selee died of the disease at the age of 49. Chance was called the "Peerless Leader." Selee's old first baseman from Boston, Fred Tenney, knew how the Cubs had turned things around, though. "Selee built the team and Chance got all the credit," he said.[6]

As Selee was putting together his team, baseball seemed in a perpetual uproar. In a game whose basic rules—nine innings, three outs, four balls, and three strikes—remained intact for a century, there was precious little stability. By 1900, a new league arrived. Angered when he was snubbed by the National League, Ban Johnson followed Hulbert's blueprint and created his own league. Johnson, sports editor of the *Cincinnati Commercial Gazette*, had turned the Western League into a profitable minor league operation and sought some accommodation from the National League (NL) for his enterprise. When they left him sitting outside a meeting room for hours and then abruptly departed without talking to him, Johnson decided the stodgy NL might be ripe for some competition. In 1900, he moved Western League franchises from St. Paul, Minnesota, and Grand Rapids, Michigan, to new markets in Chicago and Cleveland. A year later, they joined teams located in Boston, Philadelphia, Detroit, Baltimore, Washington, and Milwaukee to form Johnson's new operation.

Soon, St. Louis and New York replaced Milwaukee and Baltimore, creating an eight-team American League (AL) that would remain intact for the next half century. In five cities—St. Louis, New York, Chicago, Philadelphia, and Boston—Johnson's new league was in direct competition with entrenched NL teams. He liked it that way because it set up a dandy competition for the hearts and minds of fans.

When Johnson went shopping for players to stock his teams, he started in the rival NL where he found an ample supply of them only too happy to jump to the new league. Their enthusiasm was fueled even more when Johnson's teams discarded the NL's $2,400 salary cap. Two hundred dollars per month was a substantial salary in those days. Add a hundred or so on top of that, and the players paid attention.

The exodus was led by Hall of Famers like Cy Young, Nap Lajoie, and John McGraw, who all eagerly left NL teams for the new AL. They were followed quickly by others like Ed Delahanty, Jack Chesbro, and Wee Willie Keeler. Johnson's league was buying instant credibility by shattering the salary cap. Baseball would spend the next century trying to figure out a way to get it back.

Typical of the chaos was the case of Nap Lajoie, who jumped from the NL Philadelphia Phillies to the AL Philadelphia Athletics and won the Triple Crown in 1901, the new league's first season, leading the league in batting (.426), home runs (14), and runs batted in (125).

The Phillies were not amused and filed suit. The Pennsylvania Supreme Court ordered Lajoie back to the NL, but the order was effective only in Pennsylvania. The innovative Johnson solved that problem by simply moving Lajoie to Cleveland, where he continued to flourish. The only drawback came when the Indians traveled to Philadelphia. On those days, Lajoie hung out on the boardwalk in nearby Atlantic City.

Delahanty was another prominent Phillie who had an attack of wanderlust, especially when Johnson's league started writing those fancy checks. In 1896, he became the second player in history to hit four home runs in a game, and three years later, he won a batting championship with Philadelphia. By 1902, he found himself in Washington, lured there by $4,000—the same fee King Kelly commanded from Boston more than a decade earlier. Delahanty went on to win another batting title, the only player in history to lead each league in hitting.

By then, McGraw had jumped from the NL to the AL and back again and was running the New York Giants. Impressed by Delahanty, a .346 career hitter, he decided to go after him, offering the outfielder an extra $500 to cross back to the NL. Certainly, Delahanty was more than willing to make the jump back, but by then, weary from the player raids and the escalating salaries, the leagues had started peace talks. The established NL offered to merge with the upstarts, but Johnson was having none of that. His AL had earned its place as a Major League, and he wasn't about to abandon that status.

Peace was declared in January 1903, with the Americans recognized as a separate and equal Major League. That meant Delahanty would have to stay in Washington, barred from cashing in on McGraw's lucrative offer. It was a turn of events that left Delahanty depressed, trying to figure out why he couldn't make a bundle of money when everybody else had. He began sulking and drinking heavily, and at the end of June, with his team in the middle of a road trip, Delahanty simply failed to show up for a game in Cleveland.

That act of insubordination got him suspended, adding to his bad frame of mind. He continued traveling with the team, and on July 2, he was on the team train heading from Detroit to New York. With one too many drinks under his belt, he began threatening fellow passengers, creating a disturbance. When the train reached Niagara Falls, Delahanty was ordered off by the conductor. When last seen, he was following the train on foot as it crossed the bridge into the United States. One week later, Delahanty's body was found in the Niagara River, the most significant casualty of the war between the leagues.

In the early days of the 20th century, Pittsburgh and the New York Giants were the class of the National League. The Pirates—they got the nickname when the reckless way they recruited players from other teams was described as an act of piracy—won three straight championships from 1901 to 1903. When the Louisville franchise fell on hard times, most of its players, led by shortstop Honus Wagner, migrated to Pittsburgh. In 1903, the Pirates, equipped with three straight National League championships, played Boston in baseball's first World Series. Boston won the best-of-nine Series, five games to three.

A year later, the Series was suspended when Wagner's old basepath buddy John McGraw, by now running the New York Giants, turned his nose up at the upstart American League and refused to play its champion, Boston. He had often butted heads with umpires during his Baltimore days, leading to multiple suspensions. Snubbing the AL and the World Series in 1904 would be his revenge.

"The Giants will not play a postseason series with the American League champions," McGraw declared rather emphatically. "Ban Johnson has not been on the level with me personally and the American League management has been crooked more than once. When we clinch the NL pennant, we'll be champions of the only real major league."

Johnson fired back, saying, "No thoughtful patron of baseball can weigh seriously the wild vaporings of this discredited player who was canned from the American League."

And so, in 1904, there was no World Series.

Cooler heads prevailed the next year when the Giants repeated as National League champions, and the Series resumed with the Giants getting three shutouts by Christy Mathewson to defeat Connie Mack's AL champion Philadelphia Athletics in a best-of-seven Series for the world championship.

By then, the World Series had begun to establish itself as one of America's great annual events. And in Chicago, the Cubs were assembling a team that was about to dominate the spectacle.

2

ASSEMBLING THE DYNASTY

Even though he never played a Major League game, Frank Selee was an excellent judge of baseball talent, often moving players from one position to another like a master chess player, plotting his strategy. That skill served him well during a distinguished managing career, first in Boston and then in Chicago. His winning percentage of .598 is the fourth highest in Major League history for managers with at least 1,000 games. He won five titles in Boston and then built the Cubs into a championship club before illness forced him to leave the team just as it seemed ready to start dominating the National League.

Selee had bounced around baseball in New England, playing and managing in Cape Cod among other places and was managing in Omaha when he was summoned to Boston in 1890 to rebuild a Beaneaters team that had been stripped by defections.

In baseball's early days, players moved from team to team with abandon, and King Kelly had led an exodus of Boston players to the new Players League, leaving the Beaneaters needing a makeover. Selee rode to the rescue, replacing Jim Hart as manager. He had the great good sense to bring pitcher Kid Nichols and second baseman Bobby Lowe along with him. They became cornerstones of the Beaneaters' recovery.

Nichols would win 361 games in a 15-year career. He had seven 30-win seasons, and he completed 532 of the 562 games he started on the road to the Hall of Fame. There was no innings-count restriction on him. Lowe punctuated the 1894 season on May 30, becoming the first man to hit four home runs in a game. It was a peculiar accomplishment for the Boston leadoff batter, who managed just 71 homers in an 18-year career. He teamed with shortstop Herman Long, another Western League expatriate, to give Boston a solid up-the-middle combination. It was a formula Selee would use again.

In his second year in Boston, Selee's team won the pennant, beating out Cap Anson's Chicago White Stockings by three and a half games, the first of three straight championships for the Beaneaters. Selee and Anson were a study in contrasts. The Boston boss preferred a low-key approach, while in Chicago, the manager was a tough taskmaster.

Here's how Lowe described his manager: "He was a good judge of players. He didn't bother with a lot of signals, but let his players figure out their own plays. He didn't blame them if they took a chance that failed. He believed in place-hitting, sacrifice-hitting and stealing bases. He was wonderful with young players."[1]

The Beaneaters finished first again in 1897 and 1898 with Nichols winning 59 games over those two seasons. The first baseman was Fred Tenney, converted from catcher, a technique Selee would use again down the road. Meanwhile, in Chicago, hard times had set in. Anson's last team finished ninth, and the franchise did not fare much better over the next four years with first Tom Burns and then Tom Loftus at the helm.

Now the Cubs looked for a new direction. Selee had arrived in Boston after a player exodus, and he left after another one. The new American League created another competing market for players, and when management refused to get into a bidding war, the team went downhill. Selee was blamed for Boston's struggles and was dismissed. Jim Hart, the man he replaced in Boston, had moved on to ownership of the Chicago franchise, and armed with a new nickname, the Cubs hired Selee.

The franchise had moved through a number of identities. When a number of players defected to the rival Players League, the original White Stockings became the Remnants, a testament to what remained of their roster. They were briefly the Orphans when they were abandoned by Anson, and then the Spuds and the Colts when it occurred to Charles Sensabaugh, the sports editor of the *Chicago Daily News,* that with their roster of young players, perhaps the team should be called the Cubs. Finally, Chicago's National League team had a nickname that would stick—and, they believed, a manager who would put them back on top.

Selee was less interested in the team's name than he was in the rebuilding job he faced in Chicago. He decided to apply the same techniques he had employed in Boston. He would use a method that became a baseball axiom, building a strong team up the middle, from catcher to shortstop, second base, and center field.

When he came to town, the Cubs catcher was Frank Chance, the son of a California banker. He also played some outfield. Also available was Johnny Kling, and Selee quickly determined that Kling was the better option behind the plate. What's more, Selee needed help at first base when regular Bill Hanlon suddenly quit. Chance, an aspiring dentist before he turned to baseball, was the solution, and he was switched from catcher to first base, much the way the manager had done years earlier in Boston with Fred Tenney. That switch had worked out well, so why not use the same method in Chicago? But Chance wasn't interested in the scheme, even threatening to retire if Selee persisted with his plan. The answer turned out to be rather simple. Selee convinced management to sweeten Chance's contract. With a few extra bucks in his pocket, the former catcher was persuaded to make the move to first base. It was not an easy transition. Chance found fielding the position a challenge, much as he had catching, where his fingers were frequently beaten up from stopping pitches any way he could. But Selee stuck with him at first base because it kept his productive bat and speed in the lineup.

Kling gave the Cubs a strong defensive presence behind the plate. Equipped with a strong arm, he led National League catchers in putouts six times, and in one game against St. Louis, he threw out four base runners attempting to steal. He was a superb handler of the pitching staff headed by Mordecai "Three Finger" Brown. And he also was a skilled pocket billiards player, which would impact the Cubs some years later.

During the winter of 1909, after the Cubs had won three straight pennants, Kling won the World Pocket Billiards Championship. He left baseball for a season to defend his title. It was no coincidence that without him behind the plate, Chicago's string of titles ended that year, The next season, with Kling back in the fold, the Cubs returned to the top of the National League.

The next piece of Selee's puzzle was outfielder Jimmy Slagle, who had bounced around a number of baseball addresses in the Midwest before reaching the majors with Washington in 1899. He spent some time in Philadelphia and then in Boston with Selee. Slagle was slight, only about five foot seven and 140 pounds. But he was blessed with great speed and became an ideal leadoff hitter for Selee's Cubs. He stole 274 bases in 10 Major League seasons, including 41 in 1902 when he batted .315. Along with Chance, who was surprisingly fast for a big man, they gave the Cubs an element of speed that helped win many games. Together, they combined for 100 stolen bases in 1903, among the first National League teammates to accomplish that feat.

With Chance, Kling, and Slagle in place, Selee now set about constructing the middle of his infield. He started at shortstop where the survivor of a parade of candidates was Joe Tinker, who had been an apprentice paperhanger in his native Kansas. Tinker had been a third baseman, but once again, Selee decided on a position switch. Tinker became the shortstop against his will, and he would be a work in progress defensively, committing 141 errors during his first two Major League seasons with the Cubs.

Things improved for him defensively, though, and by 1905 he led all National League shortstops in double plays. Over the next eight years with the Cubs, he led National League shortstops in fielding percentage four times. He was a productive hitter—expert at the hit-and-run play—and he stole 336 bases over a 15-year career, all but one of them with Chicago. In 1910, he embraced an offensive weapon rarely used before. If you could steal second base and third base, why not home? And if you could steal home once, why not twice? That's precisely what he did against Cincinnati on June 28, pulling off a difficult exacta and adding another weapon to Chicago's offense.

Tinker is forever etched in the team's history because he delivered a game-winning triple over the head of New York Giants centerfielder Cy Seymour in the playoff game that decided the 1908 National League pennant. The hit came against Christy Mathewson in a season that Tinker, a career .262 hitter, batted .424 against one of the best pitchers in the history of the game.

Next, Selee added Johnny Evers to the cast. With Bobby Lowe showing signs of age, the Cubs purchased Evers, a former $4-a-week laborer in a collar factory, and inserted him at second base. On September 13, 1902, the Cubs infield had Tinker, Evers, and Chance together for the first time. Two days later, they turned their first double play against Cincinnati.

There is some evidence that the three Cubs were not really the best double-play combination in the league. Giants manager John McGraw, for one, was particularly dismissive of the Cubs infield, claiming there were plenty of other double-play combinations better than them. And unofficial statistics compiled by sportswriter Charlie Segar credited them with just 54 double plays between 1906 and 1910. But their legend was sealed by Franklin P. Adams, a columnist for the *New York Daily Mail*, who, in a rush to fill some space in his newspaper one day, composed an eight-line poem titled "Baseball's Sad Lexicon":

> These are the saddest of possible words—
> Tinker to Evers to Chance.
> Trio of Bear Cubs and fleeter than birds—
> Tinker to Evers to Chance.
> Thoughtlessly pricking out gonfalon bubble,
> Making a Giant hit into a double.
> Words that are weighty with nothing but trouble:
> Tinker to Evers to Chance.

In a 1946 letter quoted by William Hageman of the *Chicago Tribune* in 2010, Adams dismissed the poem as not very good. "I wrote that piece because I wanted to get out to the game and the foreman of the composing room at the Mail said I needed eight lines to fill," Adams wrote. "The next day (an editor) said that no matter what else I ever wrote, I would be remembered as the guy who wrote those eight lines. And they weren't very good, at that."

As good as they were on the field, Tinker and Evers had a cantankerous relationship off it. There were two incidents that caused a long rift between the Cubs second baseman and shortstop.

The trouble began in 1907, according to Evers. "We didn't even say hello for at least two years," he said. "We went through two World Series without a single word. And I'll tell you why. One day in early 1907, he (Tinker) threw me a baseball. It was a real hard ball. Like a catcher throwing to second. And the ball broke my finger. I yelled at him, 'You so-and-so!' He laughed. That's the last word we had for I don't know how long."[2]

Tinker remembered another episode that seemed to seal his sour relationship with his double-play partner. It occurred not on the field but in front of the team's hotel during a road trip and involved a taxicab.

> We dressed in the hotel and went to the ball park in hacks. Evers got into a hack all by himself and drove off, leaving me and several others to wait until the hack returned. I was mad. As soon as I got to the ballpark, I went up to him and said, "Who the hell are you that you've got to have a hack all to yourself?" One word led to another and presently we were at it, rolling around among the bats on the ball field. After we were pulled apart and it was all over, I said to Evers, "Now listen. If you and I talk to each other, we're only going to be fighting all the time. So don't talk to me and I won't talk to you. You play your position and I'll play mine and let it go at that." "That suits me," said Evers, who had a reputation for being an unpleasant sort of character. We went along two or three years without speaking.[3]

They did not allow their personal animosity to impact their play on the field. Evers offered this philosophy about his relationship with his double-play partner. "What one guy thinks about another guy on a ball team, doesn't mean a thing. That's a personal affair. What a guy thinks about the team as a whole is something else. Tinker and myself hated each other, but we loved the Cubs. We wouldn't fight for each other but we'd come close to killing people for our team. That was one of the answers to the Cubs' success."[4]

With Tinker, Evers, and Chance in place, the Cubs still needed a third baseman. The man they got was Harry Steinfeldt, who gave up a career as a traveling minstrel to play baseball. Saddled with a name that did not readily lend itself to a rhyme, Steinfeldt was destined to become the answer to a frequently asked trivia question, "Who was the third baseman on the infield of Tinker to Evers to Chance?"

The Cubs acquired Steinfeldt from Cincinnati for third baseman Hans Lobert and pitcher Jake Weimer. The new man, who had been the Reds regular third baseman for eight seasons, fit right in, batting .327 and leading the league with 176 hits and 83 runs batted in (RBIs) in 1906, his first season with Chicago.

Al Bridwell, who would hit the single that led to Fred Merkle's baserunning blunder in 1908, came up to the majors with Cincinnati in 1905, playing behind Steinfeldt. One day late in that season, Steinfeldt approached the rookie. "Kid, you're going to be the third baseman pretty soon, maybe today," he told Bridwell.[5]

Steinfeldt was prophetic. Injured later that day, he was replaced by Bridwell and never played another inning for the Reds; he was traded that winter to the Cubs.

That was the final piece to the infield Selee had begun to assemble with Tinker at shortstop, Evers at second, and Chance at first. Kling would be the regular catcher. In the outfield, the Cubs flanked Slagle with Frank "Wildfire" Schulte and Jimmy Sheckard, who was acquired from the Dodgers.

Schulte came to the Cubs in 1904 accompanied by some intriguing baggage. He favored thin-handled bats that often snapped on contact, causing him to be a favorite with bat suppliers. Then, there was his admiration for the actress Lillian Russell. When she starred in the play *Wildfire*, she threw a party for the outfielder and his teammates. In appreciation, Schulte, who owned racehorses, named one of them "Wildfire," a tribute to the actress.

Schulte also collected hairpins, believing they would translate into base hits. He scoured sidewalks, looking for discarded ones. The bigger the hairpin, he believed, the longer the hit it would create. And if the hairpin happened to be bent, why then, that predicted the direction of his hits. The theory worked for him, and Schulte flourished as a productive hitter. He led the National League in home runs in 1910 with 10 and again in 1911 when he hit 21 and drove in a league-leading 107 runs. In 1911, he also became the first player to hit four grand-slam home runs in a season and the first player to have 20 doubles, 20 triples, 20 home runs, and 20 stolen bases in a single season. It didn't happen again until Willie Mays did it in 1957. He hit for the cycle on July 20, and less than a month later, on August 15, he had a home run and a double in the same inning. His performance in 1911 earned him a Chalmers automobile, emblematic at the time of each league's Most Valuable Player. Schulte also was a daring base runner and stole home 22 times in his career.

Sheckard came to Brooklyn in 1897 and had his best season in 1901 when he batted .353 with 104 RBIs and 116 runs scored. He had a career-high 11 home runs that season, led the league with 19 triples, and punctuated his season with grand-slam home runs on consecutive days, September 23 and September 24. The Cubs acquired Sheckard from the Dodgers before the 1906 season for a package of four players, outfielders Billy Maloney and Jack McCarthy, third baseman Doc Casey, and a pitcher with the engaging name of Buttons Briggs, along with $2,000. The year before he was traded, McCarthy had a milestone game when he threw three Pittsburgh runners out at home plate on April 26, 1905, just the third time in history that had been done. It has never been duplicated. The trade with Brooklyn completed Chicago's championship outfield.

The pitching staff was next, and it already had an ace in place in the person of Mordecai "Three Finger" Brown, who came over from St. Louis in a four-player trade completed in December 1903. A farming accident when he was seven years old had cost him the index finger on his right hand. Another mishap some weeks later had broken the third and fourth fingers on the same hand, and they healed bent out of shape. So, "Three Finger" Brown really had four fingers.

Brown's disability turned into an asset. Because he gripped the ball differently to compensate, his curve ball acted differently than the type other pitchers threw, dipping like a modern-day forkball. It was a conundrum for hitters unaccustomed to seeing that kind of movement on a pitch. Brown was once asked if his hand, bent so out of shape, was a disadvantage when he pitched. "I don't know," he said. "I've never done it the other way. That old paw served me pretty well in its time. It gave me a firmer grip on the ball so I could spin it over the hump. It gave me a greater dip."[6]

Brown was the ace of the Cubs staff, and he often hooked up against Giants ace Christy Mathewson. Almost certainly the most impressive of those showdowns occurred on June 13, 1905. Both pitchers took shutouts into the ninth inning, with Brown allowing just two hits and Mathewson working on a no-hitter. The Giants bunched four hits in the ninth when they scored the game's only run. Mathewson then completed his no-hitter, winning 1–0.

Over their careers, Brown faced Mathewson 25 times, won nine in a row, and held a 13–11 edge with one no decision. Their confrontations were compelling showdowns almost every time they faced each other.

Behind Brown, the Cubs slotted Ed Reulbach, who arrived equipped with collegiate credentials after studying electrical engineering at Notre Dame and pre-med at the University of Vermont. He won 97 games in his first five seasons in the Major Leagues, with an earned run average under 2.03 in each of those years, and he had 40 career shutouts.

With pitcher Jake Wiemer sent to Cincinnati in the trade for Harry Steinfeldt, the Cubs needed a replacement. Midway through the 1906 season, the Reds supplied Orval Overall in exchange for pitcher Bob Wicker and $2,000. Wicker had been a 20-game winner in 1903 and had a remarkable victory over the New York Giants the next year when he held them hitless until the 10th inning in a 1–0 victory. But when he slumped in 1905, he was swapped for Overall, who had been 18–23 with the Reds but responded to the change in scenery by going 12–3 with Chicago.

A month after Overall was obtained, pitcher Jack Taylor, exiled to St. Louis in the "Three Finger" Brown trade, returned to the Cubs in exchange for pitcher Fred Beebe, catcher Pat Noonan, and cash. Taylor, who always insisted he was innocent when Cubs management charged him with fixing three games of the City Series against the White Sox, flourished on his return to Chicago, going 12–3 in the second half of the 1906 season after an 8–9 first half with the Cardinals. Taylor was famous for finishing what he started, throwing 186 consecutive complete games over five years and 278 complete games of his 286 career starts. There was no innings restriction on him either.

Jack Pfiester and Carl Lundgren added depth to the pitching staff with Pfiester winning 20 games in his first year and the Cubs and Lundgren winning 91 games in eight seasons in Chicago.

Selee had pieced together the nucleus of a championship team. But he was growing ill, battling a hacking cough that sometimes lingered for days. It was clear that he was gravely sick, and in the middle of the 1905 season, he had to give up his job. The diagnosis was tuberculosis. Selee moved to Denver where he died in 1909 at the age of 49.

At about the same time as Selee left Chicago, the team's first star, pitcher Albert Spalding, had moved from the playing field to the front office and then on to his flourishing sporting-goods business. Spalding's spirit of inquisitiveness led him to wonder about some serious matters. He was engaged in a long-standing debate about the origins of baseball. Sportswriter Henry Chadwick, inventor of the box score, argued that the game had its roots in England from the games of cricket and rounders. Others supported Alexander Cartwright, who laid out the original rules of the game—90 feet between bases, nine players to a team, and three outs to an inning. Then there was another faction who credited baseball's development to Abner Doubleday, the Civil War general from Cooperstown, New York. Spalding set out to get an answer, and in 1905, he created a commission headed by former National League president A. G. Mills to get to the bottom of all this. The commission sided with the Doubleday answer, although that was later disputed by other historians.

Frank Chance was Selee's replacement as manager of the Cubs, and he was less interested in baseball's origins than he was in winning games. He brought a throwback to the team, restoring Cap Anson's hard-edged approach. Consider that early on in his administration, Chance advised the Cubs, "You can do things my way or you can meet me after the game."[7]

And he meant it, too.

Chance was particularly annoyed when players on his team socialized with their opponents, shaking hands and acting as if they were old pals. "You're a ballplayer and not a society dancer at a pink tea," he scolded them. "I want to see some fight in you and not this social stuff."[8] If one of the Cubs violated Chance's rule by chatting with an opponent, it would cost the violator $10, making the casual conversation rather expensive.

Chance did not accept failure casually. When he was managing the New York Yankees, who had changed their name from the Highlanders in 1913, he often found himself on the bench next to Bill McKechnie, a nondescript reserve player. When he was asked why he spent so much time with McKechnie, Chance growled, "Because he's the only (one) on this club who knows what it's all about. Among this bunch of meatheads, his brain shines like a gold mine."[9]

A few days after that endorsement, McKechnie found himself playing second base on a muddy field. When a ball skidded past him and landed in a puddle, McKechnie lost sight of it, costing his team a run. Chance was so angry that he fined his prize pupil and shipped him off to the minor leagues.

McKechnie must have learned something though. He went on to manage in the Major Leagues for 25 years in Pittsburgh, St, Louis, Boston, and Cincinnati, winning four pennants.

As a batter, Chance crowded the plate, making him a frequent target for pitchers. In a May 30, 1904, doubleheader, he was hit by pitches three times in the first game and twice more in the second one. He was hit in the head 36 times in his career at a time long before batter's helmets were a routine part of every player's equipment. The beanings took a terrible toll, leaving him with a loss of hearing in one ear and blinding headaches that led to surgery for blood clots in 1912.

The wins and losses of a season kept Chance on an emotional roller coaster. One time, Cubs second baseman Johnny Evers, nicknamed "The Crab" for his rather unpleasant demeanor, found the manager sitting alone in a hotel lobby, looking tired and gloomy. He tried to lighten the boss's mood, to no avail.

After a few minutes, Chance looked up and observed to no one in particular, "This business is making a crab out of me."[10]

3

WHO'S HITLESS NOW?

Now, with an All-Star lineup in place, supplemented by a strong pitching staff, the Cubs were ready to make their move. The team had signaled that it would be a force, winning 93 games in 1904 and 92 the next year. But John McGraw's New York Giants ruled the National League then, winning more than 100 games, each of those years en route to a pair of pennants.

The Cubs changed all that in 1906.

Frank Chance had replaced the ailing Frank Selee as manager midway through the 1905 season and then fine-tuned the team with the trades that delivered third baseman Harry Steinfeldt and pitcher Orval Overall.

Chicago started the season rather routinely before going on a 10-game winning streak at the end of April against Cincinnati, St. Louis, and Pittsburgh. But their run was overshadowed by tragedy. On the morning of April 18, the city of San Francisco exploded. More than 3,000 people were killed and the city destroyed by an earthquake. Baseball became an afterthought because of the devastation. Fires burned for three days, destroying 490 city blocks and leaving over 250,000 people homeless. It was reminiscent of the Great Chicago Fire of 1871. Baseball responded to the tragedy by temporarily lifting New York's ban on

Sunday baseball for an exhibition game between the Philadelphia Athletics and New York Highlanders that raised $5,600 for the victims. It was a small gesture for a city that had suffered $350 million in damages.

Meanwhile, the Cubs continued to steamroll their way through the National League. John McGraw once observed, "The team that gets off to a good start wins pennants."[1] The Cubs were about to prove their longtime rival's axiom to be true. On June 7, they punctuated their intentions with a 19–0 victory over the Giants. They scored 11 of the runs against the two best Giants pitchers— Christy Mathewson, who surrendered six runs in one-third of an inning, and Joe McGinnity. Particularly impressive was the way the Cubs ganged up on Mathewson, perhaps the best pitcher in the game. Jimmy Slagle led off with a walk, and after Jimmy Sheckard and Wildfire Schulte singled, Chicago had the bases loaded with none out. One run scored on a fielder's choice. When Harry Steinfeldt singled and Joe Tinker doubled, Mathewson's day was done. The Chicago barrage continued against McGinnity. Chicago had 22 hits in the game, five of them by Schulte. A year earlier, Mathewson had thrown three shutouts in the World Series against Philadelphia and pitched a no-hitter against what was essentially the same Cubs lineup. But this was a new year as well as a statement that this Chicago team was on a mission and no one, especially not McGraw's Giants, would stand in its way.

What sealed their season, however, was a remarkable month of August when the Cubs—some holdouts were still calling the team the Spuds—went 26–3 and blew away the rest of the league. Included in the stretch were six wins in seven games against the Giants, a sort of declaration by Chicago that McGraw's club was no longer the top team in the National League. One of those wins was a forfeit when McGraw, in a fit of pique over a disputed call the previous day, ordered umpire Jim Johnstone barred from the Polo Grounds. The other umpire, Bob Emslie, refused to work alone. National League rules called for each team to supply a player to call the game if the regular umpires were unavailable. Frank Chance was having none of that. Emslie decided it was a forfeit for the Cubs, and the next day, that ruling was upheld by National League president Harry Pulliam.

Perhaps the only negative moment during the month came on August 13 when the Brooklyn Superbas knocked out Jack Taylor, who had returned from his brief exile in St. Louis, in the third inning of their game, ending an incredible streak of 187 consecutive complete games for Taylor. It hardly mattered to the Cubs, who were in the midst of another 10-game winning streak and won the game, 11–3.

The Cubs won a record 116 games that season. They were 56–21 at home and 60–15 on the road, and they finished 20 games ahead of the Giants. Pittsburgh finished third with 93 wins and was 23½ games behind. The other five teams in the league all finished 45 or more games behind the Cubs. It was a complete domination and a regular-season win total unmatched in Major League baseball for 95 years until the Seattle Mariners won 116 in 2001. Chicago's winning percentage of .800 on the road and .763 overall remain the best in modern baseball history.

This was the era of the deadball, and the Cubs were experts at small ball. They manufactured runs without much benefit of home runs. Led by Wildfire Schulte's seven home runs, the team managed a total of just 20 for the season. Compare that with the club's 283 stolen bases led by Frank Chance, who had 57, and Johnny Evers, who had 49. Jimmy Sheckard and Joe Tinker had 30 apiece. So the legendary double-play team of Tinker to Evers to Chance had 136 stolen bases that season, considerably more than the number of double plays they turned.

McGraw never bought into the Tinker-Evers-Chance mystique, often arguing that other combinations, including his own of Dave Bancroft, Frank Frisch, and George Kelly, were more proficient than the "trio of Bear Cubs." Fielding statistics were less precise in those days, but McGraw was adamant, figuring it wouldn't hurt to get under the skin of the Cubs by dismissing their heralded unit.

The newly acquired Steinfeldt was the Cubs' best hitter in 1906, batting .327, second only to Honus Wagner's .339. Steinfeldt led the league with 176 hits and 83 runs batted in (RBIs). Chance at .319 and catcher Johnny Kling at .312 were the only other .300 hitters in the lineup, but the Cubs knew how to build runs and win games. Chance used sacrifice bunts to move runners along 231 times, a Major League record for two seasons until he pushed the record to 270 in 1908. Chance played thinking person's baseball.

The pitching staff was dominant. "Three Finger" Brown had 26 victories, including 10 shutouts, and his earned run average was a miniscule 1.04. Typical of his dominant season was a game on July 4, his 30th birthday, when he hooked up with Lefty Leifield of the Pittsburgh Pirates in the opening game of an Independence Day doubleheader. Brown threw a one-hit shutout and won the game when Jimmy Slagle opened the ninth inning with the only hit off Leifield and came around to score the game's only run on an error. Leifield had the only Pirates hit against Brown. The Cubs also won the nightcap, 1–0.

Behind Brown, the Cubs had some other impressive pitchers. Jack Pfiester was 20–8 with a 1.56 ERA. Ed Reulbach was 19–4, leading the league in winning percentage and allowing just 1.65 runs per game. Carl Lungren won 17 games, and Orval Overall and Jack Taylor added 12 wins apiece. The pitching staff led the league with a stingy 1.76 earned runs per game.

Across town, the White Sox were in a much tighter race, made more difficult by a paltry offense that managed to hit just .230 for the season. But the Sox had a solid pitching staff, one that dominated the league and helped the team finish three games ahead of the New York Highlanders.

Typical of how the White Sox won games was a 19-game winning streak in August that included eight shutouts. For the season, Chicago recorded 29 one-run victories. The pitching staff was led by Frank Owen, who won 22 games, and Doc White, who went 18-6 and led the league with a 1.52 ERA. White had five straight shutouts in the September stretch run. If he had failed at baseball, he had a fallback plan, because after graduating from Georgetown University, he worked as a dentist during the off-season.

Nick Altrock, who appreciated the lighter side of baseball, went 20–13 with a 2.06 ERA. Later, he would surface as a first-base coach with the Washington Senators, entertaining fans and distracting them when their team struggled. He was a foil for Al Schacht, who won fame as the original Clown Prince of Baseball.

The fourth member of the White Sox pitching rotation was spitball specialist Ed Walsh, who, in the third season of what would become a Hall of Fame career, went 17–13 with a 1.88 ERA. Walsh, who like the Cubs' Mordecai Brown came to baseball after toiling in mines, was a workhorse, averaging 375 innings per season over a six-year span.

On September 17, 1906, as the White Sox battled New York and Cleveland in the closing days of the pennant chase, Walsh faced a Philadelphia Athletics rookie making his Major League debut. Eddie Collins, also on his way to the Hall of Fame, singled in that at-bat, but what made it notable is that he used a fictitious last name—"Sullivan"—to preserve his college eligibility at Columbia University. The hit still counted in the more than 3,000 that Collins accumulated in his career.

The way the White Sox hit that season, maybe all of them should have used aliases. Their batting averages were anemic. The leading hitter was second baseman Frank Isbell at .279. Except for third baseman George Davis, who batted .277 and led the team with 80 runs batted in, no other starter hit more than .260. Manager Fielder Jones, who played the outfield for the Sox, hit .230, which coincidentally was the team batting average for the season, lowest in the Major Leagues. Bringing up the rear were catcher Billy Sullivan at .214 and third baseman Lee Tannehill at .183. The White Sox managed seven home runs for the year. No wonder they were called the "Hitless Wonders."

It was a forgettable lineup, except for Davis, who was a productive switch-hitter throughout his Hall of Fame career, accumulating 2,660 hits and 1,437 RBIs over 20 years. But on the eve of the 1906 World Series, the White Sox's most dependable hitter came down sick. Thrust onto baseball's biggest stage, the White Sox would have to scramble without their best hitter.

Fielder Jones's solution was to move Tannehill from third base to shortstop and plug utilityman George Rohe in at third base. Rohe had batted .258 that season and like the rest of his teammates was not much of a run producer. Inexplicably, Jones placed him in the cleanup spot in the lineup. It was a long shot that paid off for the White Sox.

Frank Chance's Cubs were also missing one of their regulars. With Jimmy Slagle injured, the Cubs used Solly Hofman in center field. Hofman led off, just as Slagle had when he was in the lineup.

The hyperbole was sky high as the Series between the two Chicago rivals was set to begin. This would be the first intracity World Series, a landmark event and forerunner to the popular Subway Series that dominated New York City baseball five decades later. The two Chicago teams had never played each other before in the postseason and, as it turned out, never would again. The *Chicago Tribune* discarded journalistic standards for a little cheerleading on the day after the White Sox clinched the American League pennant, declaring, "Last night, Chicago was baseball mad." The newspaper reported, "Men stood and cheered in elevated trains when the news was passed along that the Sox were safe and Chicago had two pennants—and the world's championship."[2]

There was plenty of conversation, sometimes deteriorating into cursing and fisticuffs, and there was plenty of wagering going on in the streets of the city. Typical of the trash talk exchanged between the teams, Cubs outfielder Jimmy Sheckard, who hit just .262 during the regular season, boasted he could hit .400 against the White Sox pitchers.

Both teams had a player-manager, a penny-wise way to save a salary for penurious owners. The Cubs' Frank Chance, a bit of a grouch who did not suffer failure kindly, faced off with outfielder Fielder (that was his real name) Jones of the White Sox. Chance had a hard edge and demanded performance from his team. Jones was more understanding. He had to be, considering the paltry White Sox attack.

Chance's Cubs sometimes seemed to score at will. Jones's White Sox were more of a finesse group, often scratching out just enough runs to win. "They were a club that a manager could depend on," Jones once said. "It is true that their batting was light. But they hit at the right time. Every man knew his business. They won ballgames because they were good ballplayers and a good ballplayer can't be manufactured out of batting averages."[3]

Both managers were educated men. Chance had studied dentistry at the University of California. Jones graduated from Alfred University with a degree in engineering. So this would be a battle of wits between two sharp-minded bench bosses.

Except for Hofman replacing Slagle in center field, Chance's lineup for the opening game was identical to the one that had destroyed National League opponents that season. Jimmy Sheckard batted second followed by Wildfire Schulte and then Chance, batting cleanup. Behind the manager was the team's best hitter,

Harry Steinfeldt, and then the shortstop–second base combination of Joe Tinker and Johnny Evers. Rifle-armed catcher Johnny Kling batted eighth.

For the White Sox, right fielder Ed Hahn led off followed by manager Jones in center field and then second baseman Frank Isbell. George Rohe, replacing the injured George Davis, played third base and batted fourth, followed by first baseman Jiggs Donahue, left fielder Patsy Doherty, catcher Billy Sullivan, and the light-hitting Tannehill at shortstop.

With no days off needed for travel, the Series alternated between the Cubs' home field of West Side Park and South Side Park, home of the White Sox. For the opener on October 9, the city was in a frenzy. City Hall was closed down. Baseball ruled Chicago. With anticipation sky high but temperatures uncomfortably low, a crowd of 12,693, well below the 16,000 capacity, traveled to the Cubs' home field to watch the first game between the intracity rivals. With snow flurries in the biting autumn air, Mordecai "Three Finger" Brown took the mound to start for the Cubs against Nick Altrock of the White Sox. Altrock got the start instead of Ed Walsh because the White Sox feared the cold weather might cause their ace's signature spitball to misbehave. The pitch dated back to the end of the 19th century, but Walsh is credited with popularizing it and it was his main weapon. It was outlawed in 1920.

The two starters were perfect through three innings. Schulte had the game's first hit, an infield single, with two out in the bottom of the fourth. He reached second on an attempted steal when Isbell dropped catcher Billy Sullivan's throw for an error. But Chance left him stranded when he bounced back to the pitcher.

In the top of the fifth, George Rohe led off with a triple to left field, the first hit of the game for the White Sox. After Brown struck out Donahue, Doherty bounced back to Brown and Rohe broke for the plate. The Cubs might have had him except that Kling, the usually sure-handed catcher, dropped the throw for an error, allowing the runner to score.

In the next inning, Brown walked Altrock, the opposing pitcher, who was leading off. Walking traditionally light-hitting pitchers has always been viewed as a fatal mistake, and it wound up costing the Cubs. Altrock advanced to second on a sacrifice, and Fielder Jones followed with a single. Altrock tried to score on the hit, but Solly Hofman's throw to Kling retired the pitcher. Jones went to second on the play and then advanced to third on a passed ball by Kling and scored on a two-out single by Isbell.

Now the White Sox had a 2–0 lead, often a full game's quota of runs for the Hitless Wonders. The Cubs mounted a comeback in the bottom of the sixth. Kling, already embarrassed by two fielding blunders—the dropped throw allowing the first run to score and the passed ball setting up the second one—opened with a walk, and Brown beat out an infield hit over the mound. The runners advanced on Hofman's sacrifice and then Kling scored on a wild pitch. But Altrock retired the next two hitters, leaving the tying run stranded in scoring position. The Cubs would never threaten again as the White Sox won the World Series opener 2–1, beating Brown, the ace of the Cubs' staff.

Armed with a victory in the Series opener and heading across town to their home field, the White Sox were sky high for Game Two. The Cubs' Ed Reulbach brought them back to earth rather quickly. The Notre Dame grad allowed just one hit, and his teammates beat up White Sox starter Doc White and reliever Frank Owen in a 7–1 romp.

The Cubs jumped White for three runs in the second inning with bunt hits by Joe Tinker and Reulbach fueling the rally, which was helped along on a key error by Sox second baseman Frank Isbell. Steinfeldt's two-out RBI single made it 4–0 in the third, a deep hole for the offensively challenged White Sox. They managed an unearned run in the fifth on an error by Tinker but did not get a hit against Reulbach until Jiggs Donahue singled in the seventh. It would be the only hit Reulbach allowed this day. One hit would not get the White Sox very far on this cold, windy day, and the Cubs wrapped up the victory with a run in the sixth when Billy Sullivan's throw sailed wide on a double steal, allowing Tinker to score. Tinker's RBI-single and a wild pitch delivered two wrap-up runs in the eighth. Steinfeldt had three hits, and Tinker added a pair in the victory.

Now the Series was tied at 1–1 and headed back to the Cubs' home, West Side Park.

With the weather still cold for Game Three, the White Sox finally started Walsh, and the Cubs countered with Jack Pfiester. The two were locked in a scoreless duel through five innings. Then in the sixth, the White Sox mounted a rare rally, loading the bases with none out on a single by light-hitting Lee Tannehill, a walk to pitcher Walsh, and a hit batsman. Pfiester retired the next two batters, but then Rohe, the super sub, tripled for the second time in three games, clearing the bases. Suddenly, the run-starved White Sox had a 3–0 lead, and that was all they would need with Walsh's spitter virtually unhittable. He threw a two-hit shutout and struck out 12 Cubs hitters.

Suddenly, the Hitless Wonders were leading the World Series, two games to one.

George Davis returned to the White Sox lineup for Game Four, but Fielder Jones kept George Rohe, hero of the two Sox wins, in the lineup and benched Tannehill. Both Rohe and Davis went hitless against Mordecai Brown, who returned to the mound for the Cubs in Game Four and got them even with a brilliant two-hit shutout, beating first-game winner Nick Altrock 1–0. The game was scoreless until the seventh inning when White Sox right fielder Ed Hahn lost Frank Chance's pop fly in the sun and the ball fell for a single. Two sacrifices moved Chance to third, and

Tinker's two-out single gave Brown the only run he would need for the victory.

Now, with the Series tied at 2–2, the pivotal fifth game matched Walsh for the White Sox, coming off his two-hit shutout in Game Three, with Reulbach of the Cubs, who threw a one-hitter in his first Series start. It shaped up as another pitcher's duel, but it didn't turn out that way. Both teams came out swinging, certainly expected for the Cubs but most unlikely for the White Sox, who had had just 11 hits in the first four games but still managed to win two of them.

The Sox bunched three hits, including a double by Rohe, for a run in the first against Reulbach, but the Cubs struck back for three runs in the bottom half of the inning, two of the runs scoring on a wild throw by Frank Isbell as he tried to complete what would have been an inning-ending double play. The White Sox tied the score with two runs in the third when Davis stole home and then took charge of the game with an uncharacteristic four-run rally in the fourth with doubles by Isbell—who had a World Series record four of them in the game—and Davis and Jiggs Donahue as the key hits.

Walsh lasted six innings, and Doc White pitched the final three in an 8–6 White Sox victory. Suddenly, the Hitless Wonders were one win away from a most unlikely world championship.

Faced with a must-win Game Six, the Cubs turned again to their ace, Mordecai Brown, and supplied him with a run in the top of the first inning on an RBI double by Wildfire Schulte. But pitching on just one day's rest and for the third time in six days, Brown was shelled early and often by the suddenly robust White Sox hitters. The Sox struck quickly for three runs in the bottom of the first with doubles by Davis and Donahue doing much of the damage. Then the White Sox knocked out Brown, adding four more runs in the second with Davis's bases-loaded single driving in two of them. Ed Hahn had four hits, and George Davis and

Jiggs Donahue drove in three runs apiece. Doc White, fresh off three innings of relief the day before, went the distance in the 8–3 victory that gave the White Sox the championship in one of baseball's most unlikely World Series.

Three Sox hitters, Donahue, Isbell, and Davis, had six hits each in the Series, while Rohe had seven including two game-winning triples. Fielder Jones was proud of his team but did little to help them win, batting .095 with just two hits in 21 at-bats. For the Cubs, Schulte and Solly Hofman had seven hits each, and manager Chance added six. But Jimmy Sheckard, who boasted before the Series that he would batter White Sox pitching, went 0 for 21 and never got a ball out of the infield.

Led by Nick Altrock, who allowed just two runs and pitched a pair of complete games, four White Sox pitchers compiled a 1.50 earned run average. Brown's terrible Game Six outing left him with a bloated 3.20 ERA compared to the league-leading 1.06 that he had compiled during the regular season.

The Hitless Wonders lived up to their nickname, batting a paltry .198 for the Series. But the Cubs were worse, batting just .196.

Cubs manager Frank Chance never endured losing very well, and the 1906 World Series was no different. He was suitably outraged at the Cubs' failure, and he let his team know it.

"You're a fine bunch of stiffs," he said. "Maybe you so-and-sos learned your lesson in overconfidence and what happens when you underestimate the other so-and-sos."[4]

Meanwhile, White Sox owner Charles Comiskey was understandably thrilled with the unexpected World Series triumph and Rohe's role in the championship. In the aftermath of the victory over his crosstown rivals, the White Sox boss saluted his surprise hero. "Whatever George Rohe may do from now on," Comiskey announced, "he's signed for life with me."[5]

Rohe's White Sox life, however, turned out to be rather short. He became a regular in the Chicago lineup in 1907, and when he batted .213 he was released at the end of the season and never played another Major League game.

4

REVENGE

To a man, the Cubs were stunned at their loss in the 1906 World Series. After all, they had been heavily favored going into the Series with a much more formidable roster than the White Sox, and yet they had found a way to lose. No one was more upset with the failure than manager Frank Chance. "There is one thing I will never believe," he said when the great upset was over, "and that is the Sox are better than the Cubs."[1]

They had been beaten four times in the 1906 World Series though, so in 1907, the Cubs set out to gain some revenge. They were on a mission to prove just how good they really were. And they were really good. Once again, they proved it by beating up the rest of the National League.

Their cast of characters was largely unchanged. The infield once again had the legendary double-play combination of Joe Tinker, Johnny Evers, and Frank Chance from shortstop to second base and to first base and Harry Steinfeldt at third base. Johnny Kling was still catching with Wildfire Schulte, Jimmy Sheckard, and Jimmy Slagle in the outfield. Solly Hofman was an important spare part, who filled in capably at a number of positions. Mordecai Brown still anchored the best pitching staff in baseball. They were all but unbeatable and proved it right from the start of the season.

The Cubs opened the 1907 season on a roll, winning 23 of their first 27 games. And when they checked the standings after the first month of the season, they were in second place. That's because John McGraw's Giants went 24–3 over the same stretch. "The idea," McGraw liked to remind his team, "is to win."[2] The Cubs took their rival's advice to heart. They continued to win. The Giants, however, did not, fading to fourth place.

The Cubs did not duplicate their record 116 wins of 1906. This time they only won 107 and finished a mere 17 games in front of the Pittsburgh Pirates. The team was not exactly an offensive juggernaut. The leading hitter was manager–first baseman Chance at .293. He managed just one home run and 49 runs batted in (RBIs). Kling, the catcher, hit .284. Third baseman Steinfeldt, in his second full season in Chicago, led the team with 144 hits and 70 RBIs.

The difference for the Cubs again was the dominant pitching staff. Orval Overall went 23–7 with eight shutouts and an earned run average of 1.68. That ERA was fourth best among the Chicago starters, who produced 30 shutouts for the season. Jack Pfiester led the staff with a 1.15 ERA and went 14–9. "Three Finger" Brown went 20–6 with a 1.39 ERA. Carl Lundgren was 18–7 with a 1.17 ERA, and Ed Reulbach went 17–4 with a 1.69 ERA. The pitching staff's cumulative ERA was a remarkable 1.73, a record. Compare that with the next best showing in the National League that season, Pittsburgh's 2.30.

Typical of the summer Chicago's pitchers produced were three 1–0 victories over a five-game stretch from April 28 through May 4 against St. Louis, Cincinnati, and Pittsburgh. There were three straight shutouts from June 20 to 22 against Boston and St. Louis. First, Overall shut out the Braves 4–0 and then Brown blanked the Cardinals 2–0 for his 10th straight victory and Lundgren followed with a 3–0 shutout of the Cardinals. Reulbach gave up a run the next day to end the shutout string, but he still won the game 2–1. Then there was a doubleheader sweep against Phila- delphia on August 11, with both victories by scores of 1–0. Overall won the opener with ninth-inning help from Brown, and Reul- bach took the second game, which was shortened to seven innings so both teams could catch trains. The sweep came just over a year after Brown and Reulbach had pitched shutouts in another dou- bleheader sweep against the Phillies.

With the Giants sagging, the major competition for the Cubs came from the Pittsburgh Pirates, who had a much more potent attack and who scored the most runs in the league. Shortstop Honus Wagner led the league in four offensive categories—bat- ting (.350), stolen bases (61), on-base percentage (.408), and slug- ging percentage (.518). Wagner and teammate Ed Abbaticchio each drove in 82 runs, second best in the league. Vic Willis won 21 games, and Lefty Leifield won 20. And all that production still left the Pirates in second place at season's end, 17 games behind the Cubs.

Frank Chance remained Chicago's most combative presence. The fact that he was often the target of inside pitches and fre- quently beaned may have contributed to his prickly attitude. He was hit by pitches 137 times in his 17-year career. He had a vindictive side, as well, as illustrated by an oft-told tale concern- ing Cincinnati pitcher Jack Harper. Harper had an annoying habit of plunking Chance with pitches, once three times in a game, with the last one flush in the side of the face, knocking the Cubs manager unconscious. Chance got even in October 1906, con- vincing Cubs management to trade for Harper, cutting his salary drastically in a take-it-or-leave-it move, and then never using him, forcing the pitcher's eventual exit from Major League baseball.

Then there were the riots Chance incited, like the Joe McGin- nity affair. Never exactly pals—they would battle more than once—Chance launched a physical attack on the Giants pitcher that started a riot one day at the Polo Grounds. And in Brooklyn, fed up with rowdy fans shouting insults and hurling debris on the field, Chance picked up a bottle one day and threw it back into the seats, hitting a youngster. The resulting riot forced him to stay in the ballpark for three hours after the game and then leave with an armed escort. He also battled an occasional teammate, including most seriously, Heinie Zimmerman, who was also an irritable sort.

Joe Tinker had his moments as well: there was an episode in Cincinnati a year earlier when Tinker had his fill of a heckling fan and jumped off the team bus to confront the customer. The fan was getting the best of the battle when Tinker's teammates rescued him from the fracas.

For cantankerous behavior, though, it would be tough to top a young outfielder with the Detroit Tigers. Ty Cobb played baseball with a permanent chip on his shoulder. It is said he sharpened his spikes before games and flashed them high as he slid into bases. He simply did not care what others thought of him as long as they respected what he did in the field. And he did plenty.

Hugh Jennings, the old Orioles shortstop, had taken over as Tigers manager at the start of the 1907 season and pumped some life into a team that had finished a dismal sixth the year before. Jennings would coach third base with a whistle to keep his players on their toes. And if he happened to distract the opposing pitcher, well, so much the better. The new manager's most important move, however, was to make Cobb his full-time center fielder and slot him in the cleanup spot in the batting order, right behind Sam Crawford. With those two anchoring Detroit's attack, the Tigers led the American League with 694 runs scored. They were an offensive juggernaut.

Cobb had a huge season, batting .350 for the first of his nine straight batting championships and 12 in his career. He also led the league in hits (212), runs batted in (119), total bases (283), stolen bases (49), and slugging percentage (.468). He was an unstoppable at-bat, and he had help from Crawford, who was second in batting (.323) and second in slugging (.460). Crawford led the league with 102 runs scored and had 34 doubles and 17 triples. They formed the best 1–2 punch in baseball, and they had the same kind of bitter relationship as the Cubs shortstop–second base combination of Joe Tinker and Johnny Evers.

Cobb resented the rookie hazing that went on from veteran Detroit players. "Cobb wasn't easy to get along with," Crawford said. "Every rookie gets a little hazing, but most of them just take it and laugh. Cobb took it the wrong way. He came up with an antagonistic attitude, which in his mind turned a little razzing into a life and death struggle. He always figured everybody was always ganging up on him."[3]

Cobb summed up his attitude by saying, "To get along with me, don't increase my tension."[4]

Manager Jennings admitted that, in the beginning, he let the hazing go on to test Cobb. Once convinced that the young outfielder could not be shaken, he ordered the team to back off. "He's going to be a great baseball player and I won't allow him to be driven off this club," the manager said.[5]

Trading him, however, was a possibility.

Because of the clubhouse problems Cobb was causing, the Tigers thought about dealing him away after the 1907 season. Jennings proposed a trade with Cleveland for outfielder Elmer Flick, a low-key, productive player who was quite the opposite of Cobb in demeanor and approach to the game. Flick's statistics couldn't match Cobb's—few players could—but Jennings thought the negative baggage that accompanied Cobb might be too much to endure in the long run.

So the deal was considered—a young budding star in Cobb, coming off his first batting championship, for an older consistent

.300 hitter in Flick. In the end, Cleveland owner Charles Somers backed off the trade, believing that Cobb's fierce approach to the game was too much of a risk.

Somers's decision changed baseball history. Cobb went on dominate the game for the next two decades, accumulating a lifetime batting average of .366, the highest in Major League history, and winning 11 more batting championships. Flick developed stomach problems in spring training the next year and was limited to 9 games in 1908 and 24 games the next season before retiring from baseball.

Detroit's pitching staff in 1907 was led by Wild Bill Donovan, who went 25–4 with a 2.19 ERA. Ed Killian and George Mullin were the Tigers' other 20-game winners, but Mullin also lost 20 games, difficult to do on a team that lost only 58 all season.

Connie Mack's Philadelphia As challenged the Tigers for the American League championship with a pitching rotation headed by Eddie Plank, Jimmy Dygert, Rube Waddell, Chief Bender, and Jack Coombs. But the Tigers hung on for the title. Two years after he retired, Cobb told sportswriter Grantland Rice that his greatest thrill in baseball came in the final days of the 1907 pennant race. The Tigers were trailing the As by two runs in the ninth inning when Cobb tied the game with a home run against Waddell, one of just five he hit that season. "The game went 17 innings to a tie and a few days later, we clinched our first pennant," Cobb said. "You can understand what it meant for a 20-year-old country boy to hit a home run off the great Rube in a pennant-winning game with two outs in the ninth."[6]

Cobb was a catalyst for the Tigers. In 1907, he stole second, third, and home four times, flashing his speed to energize the Detroit attack.

After the Tigers clinched, the Cubs made sure to assemble a thorough report on their World Series opponents. In the days before the Series was to start, Chicago played a doubleheader at

St. Louis. In the opener at Robison Field, Johnny Evers was called out at third base on a close play. The Cubs protested umpire Cy Rigler's call, surrounding the umpire and refusing to give up the argument. Eventually, Rigler ran out of patience and awarded the forfeit to the Cardinals. Chicago won the second game but without manager Frank Chance or pitchers Orval Overall or Jack Pfiester, who were to start the first two games of the World Series against Detroit. The trio had traveled a couple of blocks away to Sportsman's Park to scout the Tigers, who were playing the St. Louis Browns.

That Detroit team included Germany Schaefer, one of the game's zanier characters. Schaefer did not take baseball quite as seriously as Cobb and often kept his teammates laughing with his antics. In one game, the Tigers were trailing the Chicago White Sox 2–1 with two out and a man on first in the bottom of the ninth inning. Schaefer, chatting with anybody who might care to listen at the end of the bench, was suddenly sent up to pinch hit against Doc White. No problem. Schaefer strode to the plate, made a theatrical bow to the crowd and announced that he would hit one into the left-field seats. Then he did precisely that for a game-winning home run and celebrated the feat by sliding into each of the bases. When he had completed his unusual tour of the bases, he turned to the crowd again and with his teammates in hysterics, he bowed grandly and said, "Ladies and gentlemen, thank you for your kind attention." It was one of two home runs he hit that season and one of nine that he managed in his career.

Then there was the time that Schaefer stole first base—sort of. Schaefer was on first, and Davey Jones was on third in a game against Cleveland on September 3, 1908, when the Tigers decided to try a double steal. Schaefer took off for second, but catcher Nig Clarke was having none of it, holding on to the ball and keeping Jones anchored at third.

Schaefer would not be denied. On the next pitch, he took off for first, reversing his earlier itinerary. The fans, players, and even the umpires were a little dumbfounded at this maneuver, but it worked. Now, back at first, Schaefer took off for second again on the next pitch. This time he drew the throw he wanted from Clarke and slid in safely while Jones scampered home.

It was not exactly an original stunt. Fred Tenney of the Giants did the same thing against St. Louis just over a month earlier, and Schaefer tucked the maneuver away in his memory bank, determined to try it himself if the opportunity occurred. When it did, he did.

With Schaefer's lighthearted approach to the game in sharp contrast to the cutthroat attitude of Cobb, it was strange that the two Tigers teammates should come up with the same question on the eve of the 1907 World Series against the Cubs. The Series was still in its infancy then, with the proprietors of baseball feeling their way. Before the Tigers–Cubs Series began, the ruling National Commission—there was not yet a commissioner in charge—announced that players would share gate proceeds only from the first four games. Schaefer and Cobb asked what would happen if a game ended in a tie. Since that had never happened before, the commission had not considered that remote possibility. The issue was solved quickly. If there were tie games, the players would share in those receipts as well.

Cobb and Schaefer tucked that piece of information away for future reference. It would turn out to come in very handy for the Tigers.

Meanwhile, Detroit manager Hugh Jennings delivered some pre-Series hyperbole, boasting, "I believe the Tigers are the best baseball team the world has ever seen."

He would soon encounter a better one.

In the opening game of the Series, Tigers ace Wild Bill Donovan faced Chicago's Orval Overall. The Cubs grabbed a lead in the bottom of the fourth inning when Chance led off with a walk. He advanced on a sacrifice by Harry Steinfeldt and scored on a single by Johnny Kling. When Kling tried to stretch his hit into a double, he was thrown out. It was an important out because Johnny Evers followed with a single that might have meant another run for Chicago. And on this day, runs would prove to be very scarce.

Overall protected the slender lead into the eighth inning. With one out, Davey Jones singled and stole second to put the tying run in scoring position. Then Joe Tinker fumbled Germany Schaefer's grounder for an error, giving the Tigers two base runners. Sam Crawford doubled them home and reached third when Kling dropped the throw to the plate. Claude Rossman's sacrifice fly scored Crawford for a 3–1 Detroit lead.

Could the Cubs, widely viewed as the best team in baseball, be headed for another World Series disappointment like the 1906 debacle against the White Sox? Chicago trailed 3–1 going to the bottom of the ninth inning. Detroit's Bill Donovan was three outs away from winning the opener when Frank Chance led off with a single and Harry Steinfeldt was hit by a pitch, putting the tying runs on base. After Kling popped out, Tigers third baseman Bill Coughlin kicked Johnny Evers's grounder loading the bases. Chance scored on a grounder by Wildfire Schulte, making it 3–2. Del Howard pinch hit for Joe Tinker, and Donovan struck him out for what should have been the game's last out. But Tigers catcher Boss Schmidt neglected to catch the final strike, and as the ball rolled to the backstop, Steinfeldt dashed home with the game-tying run.

Immediately, Cobb and Schaefer remembered the rule set down before the Series: players share in tie-game receipts. And here they were, tied in the opening game. Suspicious? Perhaps.

The teams played three more innings with the Tigers never threatening. Every time the Cubs came close to scoring, the deadlock was preserved. An interference call on Steinfeldt as Sheckard tried to score from third ended the 10th inning. When the Cubs loaded the bases in the 11th, Zimmerman struck out and pitcher Ed Reulbach, working in relief of Overall, rolled out. In the 12th, Sheckard was on first when Chance lined out to Germany Schaefer. Sheckard took off and was doubled off first base, ending the inning and, with darkness rolling in, the game.

If Cobb and Schaefer were smiling at each other, there was a good reason. A tie game hurt neither team and benefitted the players.

Now that the strange opener was out of the way, the teams got down to business.

Game Two did not start well for Chicago when leadoff man Jimmy Slagle was involved in one of baseball's most embarrassing plays. The Cubs were anxious to get a quick start after Slagle led off with a walk. Chicago had stolen seven bases against Detroit catcher Boss Schmidt in the opener, and the Cubs weren't about to stop running against his replacement, Fred Payne, in Game Two. Almost immediately, Slagle took off for second base and reached third when Payne's throw was wild. Now the Cubs were poised to strike early. As Slagle stood at third—he had also stolen two bases in the opener—Tigers third baseman Bill Coughlin casually strolled over to the bag. When Slagle stepped off the base, Coughlin produced the ball and tagged the runner out, executing the only hidden-ball trick in World Series history. Chance, who was at bat at the time, could not have been amused, especially after he singled and stole second. But Harry Steinfeldt struck out, and the Cubs' threat against Tigers starter George Mullin came up empty.

Pfiester gave up a run in the top of the second when Claude Rossman led off with a triple and scored on Fred Payne's single. It would, however, be the only run Detroit managed. Pfiester battled through a complete game, allowing nine hits. But the

Cubs won 3–1, scoring a run in the second on a bases-loaded walk to Tinker and two more in the fourth when Slagle singled home Tinker, stole second, and scored on Jimmy Sheckard's double.

It was the beginning of Slagle's recovery from the embarrassment of being victimized by the hidden-ball trick. He was suitably red-faced for his blunder, the kind of mistake that can linger for a player. But he made up for that terrible moment. He led all Chicago hitters in the Series with four runs batted in, scored the winning run in the deciding fifth game, and stole six bases, a record for a five-game World Series.

Ed Reulbach dominated Detroit in Game Three, limiting the Tigers to six hits, winning 5–1, and driving in a run with a single in a three-run Cubs fourth-inning rally. Johnny Evers had three hits and an RBI for Chicago.

Now the Cubs were halfway home in their quest to become World Series champions. Next, it was Orval Overall's turn. He surrendered a run in the fourth when Ty Cobb tripled and scored on a single by Rossman. The Tigers loaded the bases, but Overall struck out Charley O'Leary to end the threat. Then, an inning later, the Cubs pitcher singled home two runs and was on his way to a five-hit, 6–1 victory.

The Cubs went for the kill with their best pitcher. Mordecai Brown did not disappoint, pitching a seven-hit shutout and winning 2–0. It was the fourth straight complete game victory for Cubs pitchers, a microcosm of how they had dominated National League hitters throughout the regular season. They held Detroit's two best hitters in check throughout the Series. Sam Crawford batted .238, and Ty Cobb batted .200.

And even though they still weren't talking to each other, Joe Tinker and Johnny Evers combined to embarrass Cobb even more by arranging a pickoff of the Tigers star in the last game without even exchanging a word.

"Cobb was on second," Evers said. "Johnny Kling was catching for us. Cobb took his lead and Tinker said to him 'Don't get too far away from that bag or (Kling) will nip you off.' With that, he gave me a signal to take the throw. Cobb turned to sneer at Tinker and as he did, I rushed to cover. Kling threw the ball. We caught Cobb by two feet. It helped win the game and the Series."[7]

In the five games, the Cubs stole a record 18 bases, and the best pitching staff in baseball allowed just six runs, only four of them earned. The disappointment of 1906 was forgotten. At last, the Cubs of Tinker to Evers to Chance were world champions.

Meanwhile, Albert Spalding's investigation into the origins of baseball, born of a continuing debate with sportswriter Henry Chadwick, reached its conclusion, and the Mills Commission announced its finding at the end of 1907. The two-year investigation was conducted by a distinguished panel that included two U.S. senators and several baseball executives. The most persuasive piece of evidence came in the form of a letter from Abner Graves, a mining engineer from Denver, Colorado, who reported that Abner Doubleday had invented the game in 1839 in Cooperstown, New York, when he supposedly traced the first baseball diamond. Graves knew this, he said, because he was there. The fact that he was five years old at the time should not matter. Nor should the fact that Doubleday may never have been in Cooperstown.

Graves's testimony was somewhat flimsy evidence, but by the end of 1907, it was good enough for the commission, which declared that Doubleday, who had served at Fort Sumter in 1861 and fired the first Union gun there, was indeed responsible for launching baseball. Others were not so convinced, and they included Branch Rickey, who later would revolutionize the game by signing its first African American player. Noting the general's military service, Rickey dryly observed, "The only thing Abner Doubleday ever started was the Civil War."[8]

It should be noted that Spalding, Chadwick, and Rickey are all honored with plaques in the Hall of Fame in Cooperstown, New York. Doubleday is not.

5

ONCE MORE WITH FEELING

Take me out to the ballgame
Take me out with the crowd
Buy me some peanuts and Cracker Jacks
I don't care if I never get back
Let me root, root, root for the home team
If they don't win it's a shame
For it's one, two, three strikes you're out
At the old ballgame.

In the summer of 1908, Jack Norworth wrote the words, and Albert Von Tilzer put them to music, creating the song that has been embraced as baseball's anthem for over 100 years and is sung religiously during the seventh inning at every Cubs game in Wrigley Field. Neither man ever saw a baseball game, but they were intrigued by the interest the sport was generating around America. So their collaboration provided baseball with a catchy ditty that would serve the game well for over a century. And it's been just as long since the Chicago Cubs repeated the world championship they won that season.

The 1907 World Series triumph left the Cubs feeling pretty good about themselves. There was an aura of retribution, a sense that the disappointment of 1906 had been nothing more than an anomaly, erased once and for all from the team's memory bank.

They had some surprises in store for themselves.

First, there would be no cakewalk through the National League this season. The Pirates and Giants were loaded and would challenge Chicago for the top spot in the league all season. In mid-August the Cubs were in third place. They then won nine straight and 12 of 13 and were still in third place. That's because the Pirates and Giants had multiple weapons, more than enough talent to win their share of games. And the three-way tug-of-war ended with one of baseball's most memorable incidents, a base-running blunder that saddled 19-year-old Fred Merkle of the Giants with blame for the rest of his life.

The combative Heinie Zimmerman, starting his first full season with the Cubs, was the Opening Day hero, delivering a pinch single in the 10th inning to drive in the winning run in a 6–5 victory at Cincinnati. Zimmerman could always hit. Some would argue he won the first modern Triple Crown in 1912 when he led the league in batting at .372 and hit 14 home runs. Some accounts credit him with 103 runs batted in (RBI) and the Triple Crown. Others claim he only drove in 99 runs, three behind league leader Honus Wagner.

Not yet a regular, Zimmerman would still have a major impact on the Cubs season in 1908 but not in a positive way. He was an equal-opportunity brawler, and although manager Frank Chance was a favorite adversary, he went at it in another clubhouse battle that turned dangerous. On June 2, he was trading insults with outfielder Jimmy Sheckard. One thing led to another, and eventually Zimmerman picked up a bottle of ammonia and hurled it at the outfielder. It shattered in Sheckard's face, nearly blinding the left fielder. Chance went right after Zimmerman and was decked before the rest of the Cubs jumped in to pummel Zimmerman. Sheckard and Zimmerman wound up in the hospital and were sidelined for a month. Chance came out of the fracas with two black eyes.

The injuries to Sheckard and Zimmerman were part of a series of mishaps that often stripped the Cubs of important pieces of their team. Before Zimmerman nearly blinded him, Sheckard went down with sore ribs and then a sprained ankle. Solly Hofman, a useful reserve, had a bad knee. At various times, Johnny Evers was hurt and so was Wildfire Schulte. Pitcher Orval Overall missed a month with a pulled muscle in his rib cage.

One important player did not get hurt though. Mordecai Brown was in top form, winning 29 games, nine of them shutouts, and pitching to a 1.47 earned run average. He was not, however, the best pitcher in the league. The Giants had Christy Mathewson, who won 37 that year, 11 of them shutouts.

But Brown had plenty of help. Ed Reulbach won 24 games with seven shutouts and led the league with a winning percentage of .774. Overall won 15 games and led the league with almost seven strikeouts per game. Jack Pfiester won 12 games, but his most memorable outing may have been a no-decision. He threw a 17-inning complete game 1–1 tie against Boston. Vive Lindaman of the Braves also went the distance that day in an age when pitchers weren't pampered and their workloads were often extreme.

The Cubs battled through the injuries, and two months into the season, they were in first place, exactly where they expected to be. What they didn't expect, however, was having the Giants and Pirates right on their heels. Christy Mathewson was on a roll, headed for the winningest season of his career with the Giants, and Honus Wagner was well on his way to the sixth of his eight batting championships with the Pirates.

One of Brown's shutouts came in a 1–0 win over the Giants when he outdueled Mathewson and won the game on a home run by Joe Tinker, who always hit Mathewson well. A career .262 hitter, Tinker somehow had a career average of .350 against Mathewson and batted .400 against him in 1908. His uncanny ability to solve the Giants ace when few others could would serve the Cubs well again, later in the season.

A bit of comic relief came during the dog days of the season on August 21 when Gabby Street, a catcher for the Washington Senators, engaged in a strange stunt. For some unknown reason, Street agreed to catch a ball dropped from the top of the Washington Monument, a distance of 555 feet. The first 12 attempts went awry, but Street gathered in number 13. If Street could catch that ball, why certainly the Cubs could win another championship. It was not simple, however. But then, neither was Street making that catch.

As the pennant race hurtled through September, the Cubs, Giants, and Pirates were often separated by no more than percentage points. A loss would sometimes tumble one of them from first to third. That's how tightly they were bunched and why a doubleheader between New York and Chicago on September 22 was so crucial. The Cubs won the opener 4–3 as Brown saved the victory with two and a third innings of relief. Then Brown threw a complete game in the 3–1 second-game victory. Now the Cubs were just six percentage points behind New York, with Pittsburgh third, one and a half games back.

The next day, the Cubs and Giants were tied at 1–1 in the bottom of the ninth inning, with Moose McCormick on third base and Fred Merkle on first. Merkle was a raw rookie, a 19-year-old who was making his first start of the season, spelling Fred Tenney, who had a sore back. He had played some semipro football at Toledo, before showing up at the Polo Grounds. John McGraw liked his potential and kept him on the roster as a seldom-used backup. Now, in the ninth inning of a crucial game, the backup was to surface front and center.

With McCormick on third and Merkle on first, Al Bridwell delivered the apparent game-winning hit, scoring McCormick. But when Merkle failed to run to second, peeling off the basepaths instead and heading to the clubhouse in the custom of the day, Johnny Evers retrieved the ball and stepped on second for what he claimed was the force-out, ending the inning.

Or did it?

Bridwell's hit set off a celebration on the field, but Evers, a keen student of the rulebook, had a last gasp. He appealed to umpire Hank O'Day, who had been through a similar episode with Evers a few weeks earlier in Pittsburgh. O'Day upheld the second baseman's claim. Merkle was called out on a force play and bedlam broke out. It was impossible to continue the game.

The irony was that it wasn't clear that Evers ever had the game ball. Giants pitcher Joe McGinnity saw what the Cubs' second baseman was up to and had scrambled after the relay from center fielder Solly Hofman. He appeared to get the ball and heave it into the stands. No matter. Evers came up with a ball and stepped on second, and O'Day made the call.

Most of the fans had no idea what had happened, but with hundreds of them swarming over the field, there would be no chance for play to resume. O'Day ruled the game a tie, rather irritating McGraw. "That dirty son of a bitch," McGraw roared. "O'Day is trying to rob us of a game. How the hell did he know Merkle didn't touch second? He was at home plate and never saw a damn thing. The damn ball was out in center field."[1]

Quickly, the whole mess, termed by the *New York Times* as "considerable stupidity," landed in the lap of National League president Harry Pulliam, a low-key executive with no stomach for controversy. Bob Emslie, the base umpire, tried to help out by sending a letter to Pulliam to explain what had happened. His testimony, discovered years later in a box of uncataloged material in the Hall of Fame by baseball historian John Thorn, was crucial.

"As my back was turned to that play, watching Bidwell," Emslie wrote, "I did not know if Merkle had run to second or not but as my attention was called to it, I looked out in right field and saw

Merkle going toward the clubhouse and McGinnity was down at second base scrambling with Evers to get the ball away from him."

McGraw was angry but did not blame Merkle for the affair, arguing that the young man was only doing what most players did in that situation. When he became aware that the Cubs protest had reached Pulliam's desk, the Giants manager took action. He had his players sign affidavits swearing that Merkle had touched second base legally. Then he called Merkle and dispatched him to the Polo Grounds that night, armed with a lantern and orders to touch second base. That way, the manager reasoned, if Merkle were ever called to testify about the affair, he could honestly say that on September 23, he had indeed touched second base.

Nice try.

Pulliam moved swiftly to resolve the issue. First, he dismissed protests from both teams—the Giants claiming they had won fair and square and the Cubs claiming it should have been a forfeit. The Cubs, in fact, even showed up early on September 24, intending to play a doubleheader to make up for the game they claimed was a tie. When the Giants and the umpires were not on hand for the phantom game, Chicago claimed a forfeit.

Pulliam was having none of that either. The teams would play out the schedule starting that day with the regularly scheduled late-afternoon game. The Giants charged out to a 5–0 lead, but when the Cubs staged a seventh-inning comeback against New York starter Hooks Wiltse, McGraw went right back to his ace. Christy Mathewson had pitched nine innings the day before but came back to save the 5–4 victory.

Pulliam ruled that the Merkle game was a tie to be replayed at season's end if the outcome impacted the pennant race.

And it did.

Baseball was still buzzing over the Merkle game and the ensuing turmoil when Chicago's Ed Reulbach took things in his own hands and delivered an exclamation point to the frantic September pennant race. Three days after the Merkle game, the Cubs sent Reulbach out to pitch the first game of a doubleheader in Brooklyn. He responded with a five-hit shutout, striking out seven as Chicago won the opener, 5–0.

In the second game, manager Frank Chance trotted Reulbach right back to the mound, and this time he was even better, limiting Brooklyn to three hits with four strikeouts and winning 3–0. Both games had been close. The Cubs led the opener 1–0 after six innings before scoring four times in the last three innings. The nightcap was 1–0 into the eighth inning.

The double shutout was achieved in 2 hours, 52 minutes, less time than it often takes modern baseball to complete a single game. There have been 24 pitchers who have thrown two complete game victories in a single day, but Ed Reulbach is the only one who threw shutouts in both games.

The doubleheader shutouts came in the midst of a streak of 44 scoreless innings by Reulbach, who was every bit as vital to the Cubs pitching rotation as "Three Finger" Brown. He had 25 complete games in a 24–7 season, but one of his losses was the result of an old baseball superstition that striking out the first batter would be bad luck for a starting pitcher. The belief was it would be fine to retire the leadoff man on a fly ball or a groundout. But a strikeout of that first hitter would mean trouble.

So on August 13, when Reulbach got two quick strikes on Pittsburgh's Roy Thomas leading off, the Cubs starter did not throw another strike to him. Thomas wasn't biting at bad pitches and walked. He advanced to second on a sacrifice and scored on a single. The run held up for a 1–0 Pirates victory that could prove crucial in the tight pennant race that was developing among Pittsburgh, New York, and Chicago.

Reulbach's 24th victory of the season was a cakewalk, 16–2 against Cincinnati on October 3. That win left the Cubs one-half game behind Pittsburgh and one game ahead of the Giants in the three-way pennant race. The next day, more than 30,000 fans squeezed into the West Side Grounds, the largest baseball crowd in Chicago history to that date, to watch the Cubs play the Pirates. The game was tied at 2–2 in the sixth inning when Joe Tinker doubled with two out. The Pirates walked Johnny Kling to get to the pitcher, but Brown crossed up the strategy with an RBI single, scoring the go-ahead run in what became a 5–2 victory for Chicago and eliminated the Pirates.

However, urban legend reportedly put the outcome into question. In the ninth inning, with a runner on first, Pittsburgh's Ed Abbaticchio hit a ball into the right-field stands. Umpire Hank O'Day, already famous for the Merkle affair, called it foul, despite protests by the Pirates that it was fair and should have been ruled either a double or a home run, fueling a Pittsburgh rally. A few months later, a woman fan is alleged to have filed suit, claiming she was injured by Abbaticchio's ball. And by the way, she said, she was sitting in fair territory.

No evidence was ever uncovered to support the claim, and there is some suspicion that the story is apocryphal. For their part, the Cubs never looked back. They were now in first place.

The outcome left fans in a frenzy. They rushed the field and carried the players off like so many conquering heroes. But the pennant race was not over. The win pushed the Cubs into first place at 98–55 and finished the Pirates at 98–56. But the Giants were still alive at 95–55 with three games remaining against the Braves. Sweep Boston and New York would force a playoff against the Cubs.

John McGraw's team delivered, winning all three games against the Braves to finish tied with Chicago. The Merkle matter would be resolved in a one-game playoff for the pennant with Jack Pfiester pitching for the Cubs against Giants ace Christy Mathewson.

Fans were going crazy over the frenetic finish to the season. Thousands slept outside the Polo Grounds to make sure they would see the decisive game. On a warm day, more like August than October, a crowd of 50,000 jammed the ballpark, and many more watched from the slopes above the field called Coogan's Bluff. A New York City fireman, Henry McBride, scrambled precariously up to the elevated train tracks that looked down on the field, lost his footing, and tumbled to his death. The tragedy did not deter others who were quick to follow McBride's path, ignoring the dangers. Another fan fell from his perch, suffered a broken leg, and pleaded with emergency workers to let him stay for the game. Police used fire hoses to control the overflow crowd that packed the oddly shaped ballpark on the northern tip of Manhattan.

Before the game ever started, there was considerable gamesmanship at work. There were rumors that the game might be fixed, and McGraw kept the Giants on the field longer than permitted, cutting into the Cubs' batting practice time. Angry words were exchanged. Giants pitcher Joe McGinnity and Cubs manager Frank Chance got into an ugly scuffle. Cubs players received death threats that suggested organized crime might have an interest in the outcome. The Polo Grounds was rapidly deteriorating from a place hosting a pastoral game of baseball into a raucous madhouse, more appropriate for a prizefight.

Cubs starter Jack Pfiester had beaten the Giants three times in 1908 but never made it out of the first inning this time. He hit Fred Tenney with his first pitch and then walked Buck Herzog. After Roger Bresnahan struck out, catcher Johnny Kling caught Herzog napping and picked him off first base. Now, with a chance to get out of the inning, Pfiester surrendered a double to Mike Donlin, scoring Tenney. That was enough for Cubs manager Frank Chance. He brought in his ace, "Three Finger" Brown, to replace Pfiester. Brown, pitching for the 11th time in 14 days, struck out Art Devlin to end the inning. But the Giants had the lead, and they had Mathewson on the mound.

In the Cubs' third inning, Joe Tinker led off and sent a ball beyond the reach of New York center fielder Cy Seymour. Mathewson had motioned for Seymour to play deeper, but the center fielder either didn't see the sign from his pitcher or chose to ignore it. In any event, Chicago had the tying run on third base. Johnny Kling delivered the RBI single that tied the game. Now, with Mathewson on the ropes, the Cubs mounted the decisive rally. After a sacrifice and a fly out, Johnny Evers walked. Wildfire Schulte singled for one run, and Frank Chance doubled for two more. Suddenly, Chicago had a 4–1 lead. That was plenty for Brown. He surrendered one more run but earned his 29th victory of the season and 9th straight against Mathewson.

Chicago's victory led to mayhem on the field as angry fans rushed the Cubs. Chance was decked by a punch to the neck that shattered cartilage and left him gasping for breath. Solly Hofman was hit in the face by a pop bottle. Police with revolvers drawn had to escort the Chicago players off the field.

The drama didn't end there. There were reports that someone associated with the Giants had approached umpire Bill Klem before the game with a proposed bribe to fix the game. Klem was above reproach, but when the rumors persisted National League president Harry Pulliam ordered an investigation. Klem testified in December that Dr. Joseph Creamer, who worked for the Giants, had stopped him before the game, waving a fistful of money. According to Klem, Creamer said, "Here's $2500. It's yours if you will give all the close decisions to the Giants and see that they win sure. You know what is behind me and you needn't be afraid of anything. You will have a good job for the rest of your life."[2] Creamer denied the allegation, but Pulliam believed the umpire and the Giants decided to turn elsewhere for their medical care. The doctor was barred from baseball for life.

Merkle was miserable over the affair and wanted to quit baseball. McGraw talked him out of that with a $500 raise for 1909,
and the first baseman went on to a productive 16-year career in
which he batted .273 and stole 272 bases, swiping home 11 times.
He even managed some small payback on Evers, pulling the hidden-ball trick on him when he stepped off first base in a game two
years after the bonehead play that many believe cost the Giants
the pennant in 1908.

The bottom line, though, was the Cubs were National League
champions for the third straight time, not by the 20- and 17-game
margins of the previous two seasons, but National League champions nevertheless.

In the American League, the Detroit Tigers had repeated as
champions in a tight three-way race, edging Cleveland and Chicago for their second straight pennant. And now, they would face
the Cubs again in the World Series. Once again, Detroit's main
weapon was the mercurial Ty Cobb, who led the American
League in hits, doubles, triples, and RBIs.

The Cubs were still running on adrenaline when they traveled
to Detroit to start the Series just two days after they had dispatched the Giants. The Tigers were determined to put up a
better fight than they had the year before, and they did—for a
while.

Game One was played in a rainstorm, with the field muddied
and looking more like a swamp than a baseball diamond. After
Cobb drove in a run in the first inning, the Cubs ganged up on
Detroit starter Ed Killian for four runs in the third inning, bunch-
ing four hits and capitalizing on a couple of Tigers errors. Ed
Reulbach was cruising with a 5–1 lead after six innings, but suddenly it all came apart. The Tigers rallied for three runs in the
seventh in a rally started on hits by Cobb and Claude Rossman.
Red Downs's double and a single by pitcher Ed Summers, who
had relieved Killian, finished Reulbach.

Orval Overall hit the first batter he faced but then escaped further damage in the seventh. When he walked Sam Crawford leading off the eighth, Chance went to Brown again. But errors by Chance and Johnny Evers led to two runs, and Detroit was in front 6–5 going to the ninth. That's when Summers, who had won 24 games in the regular season, ran out of gas. The Cubs bunched six straight hits in a rally started by Wildfire Schulte's single and spiced by a double steal by Solly Hofman and Joe Tinker to score five runs and seize the lead and the game. Chance, Harry Steinfeldt, Hofman, Tinker, and Kling had the other hits to turn the game Chicago's way. Jimmy Sheckard had three hits, two of them doubles, for the Cubs.

The Series moved to Chicago for Game Two, and this one was in sharp contrast to the free-scoring opener. Overall, fresh off his shaky three-batter relief appearance the day before, started for Chicago against Wild Bill Donovan. The game was scoreless until the eighth inning when Hofman reached on an infield single and Tinker followed with a wind-blown home run, the first World Series homer since 1903. Shaken by the homer, Donovan then gave up four more runs in the inning on a double by Kling, singles by Sheckard and Evers, and a triple by Schulte. The Tigers scored a meaningless run in the ninth on an RBI single by Cobb as Overall completed the four-hitter and the Cubs were halfway to another championship.

In Game Three, the sheer willpower of Cobb carried the Tigers to their first victory in two years of trying against the Cubs. Chicago had grabbed a 3–1 lead against Detroit starter George Mullin, but the Tigers came off the deck, scoring five runs in the sixth inning against Jack Pfiester on their way to an 8–3 victory. Mullin started the rally by drawing a walk. The Tigers followed with five straight singles and a double by Ira Thomas to take the lead. Cobb had four hits in the game, drove in two runs, and stole two bases.

The Tigers never scored another run in the Series. "Three Finger" Brown shut Detroit out 3–0 on four hits in Game Four, with RBI singles by Steinfeldt and Hofman supplying him with an early lead and an error by Cobb allowing a wrap-up run in the ninth inning.

Next, it was Overall again, this time throwing a three-hitter and outpitching Wild Bill Donovan as the Cubs finished off the Tigers 2–0. Chance delivered the first run with an RBI single in the first inning, and Johnny Evers doubled home Chicago's other run in the fifth. Detroit fans, perhaps sensing the inevitable, stayed away from Game Five with just 6,210 showing up, the smallest attendance for a game in World Series history. It was over quickly, too, lasting just one hour, twenty-five minutes, the shortest World Series game ever.

For the second straight year, Chicago had beaten Detroit in five games. Frank Chance led his team with a .429 batting average. Wildfire Schulte hit .389, Johnny Evers hit .350, and Solly Hofman, filling in for the injured Jimmy Slagle, batted .316. Brown and Overall each won two games, and each threw a shutout. The only offense the Tigers could muster came from Cobb, who batted .368, wiping out the memory of his dreadful .200 Series batting average the year before. But no other Detroit regular batted more than Sam Crawford's .238, which matched his average from the 1907 World Series.

Once again, the Chicago Cubs were world champions. No one ever thought it would be the last time.

Meanwhile, the Merkle affair took a terrible toll on Harry Pulliam. He fell into a deep depression and suffered a nervous breakdown in February 1909, forcing him to take a leave of absence. He returned to his post the following June, seemingly in better spirits. But on July 25, 1909, 10 months after Fred Merkle failed to touch second base, Pulliam left his dinner table at the New

York Athletic Club, where he lived, went to his room, put a revolver to his head, and pulled the trigger.

He died the next day.

Actor Joe Mantegna (shown here rooting for slugger Hank Sauer) became a Cubs fans as a child growing up in Chicago and remains one today. Courtesy of Joe Mantegna.

Managers John McGraw of the Giants and Frank Chance of the Cubs battled each other throughout the decade of the Last Chicago Cubs Dynasty. Library of Congress Print and Photographs Division, Washington, DC.

ADRIAN C. ANSON.
ALLEN & GINTER'S
RICHMOND. Cigarettes. VIRGINIA.

Cap Anson was believed to be the first player to accumulate 3,000 hits and was the winningest manager in Cubs history, leading the team to five pennants before the turn of the 20th century. Library of Congress Print and Photographs Division, Washington, DC.

Albert Spalding was lured to the new Cubs National League team in 1876 and won 47 games. Library of Congress Print and Photographs Division, Washington, DC.

Frank Schulte had the nickname "Wildfire" because of his affection for the actress Lillian Russell, who was one of his biggest fans and appeared in a play with that name. Library of Congress Print and Photographs Division, Washington, DC.

Jimmy Sheckard combined speed and power to be an offensive force for the Cubs, leading the league in home runs with nine in 1903 and tying Frank Chance for the lead in stolen bases with 67. Library of Congress Print and Photographs Division, Washington, DC.

A baserunning blunder by rookie Fred Merkle became the turning point in the 1908 pennant race and helped the Cubs win the pennant and capture their last World Series championship. Library of Congress Print and Photographs Division, Washington, DC.

Ed Reulbach was the only pitcher in baseball history to throw shutouts in both games of a doubleheader on September 26, 1908, against Brooklyn. Library of Congress Print and Photographs Division, Washington, DC.

Orval Overall relied on a sweeping curveball as the Cubs' opening-day pitcher every year from 1906 to 1910. He compiled a record of 3–1 with a 1.75 earned run average in four World Series. Library of Congress Print and Photographs Division, Washington, DC.

Joe Tinker was the first cog in the famous Tinker-to-Evers-to-Chance double-play unit and was a lifetime .262 hitter but batted .350 against Christy Mathewson. Library of Congress Print and Photographs Division, Washington, DC.

Mordecai "Three Finger" Brown was injured in a farming accident as a child but still became a Hall of Fame pitcher with 239 wins and was leader of the staff during the Last Chicago Cubs Dynasty. Library of Congress Print and Photographs Division, Washington, DC.

Johnny Evers was a student of the baseball rulebook and caught rookie Fred Merkle's baserunning blunder in one of the most significant events of the 1908 pennant race. Library of Congress Print and Photographs Division, Washington, DC.

6

104 WINS ARE NOT ENOUGH

In the winter of 1908, a few months before the 1909 season, the Chicago Cubs were on top of the baseball world. They had won three straight National League pennants. They were the defending World Series champions. They had a formidable roster that included the legendary double-play unit of Joe Tinker, Johnny Evers, and Frank Chance and the best pitching staff in baseball headed by Mordecai "Three Finger" Brown.

And then trouble began to develop.

The Cubs catcher was Johnny Kling, a master at handling pitchers and distracting hitters. Kling would keep up a steady line of chatter with batters, a habit that earned him the nickname "Noisey." He liked to talk to umpires, too, and some believed it was all part of a psychological plan to get an edge on ball-strike decisions. He was blessed with a rifle arm and loved to put it on display. One day in 1907, he threw out four St. Louis runners trying to steal second base. In the World Series that year, he cut down 7 of 14 Detroit runners attempting to steal. The next year, he threw out 11 Tiger runners. In two World Series confrontations against Kling, the mercurial Ty Cobb, who stole 892 bases in his career, managed just two steals. Kling was widely believed to be the best catcher in baseball. The problem for the Cubs was that he was also a world champion billiards player.

When Kling won the pocket billiards world title following the 1908 World Series, the catcher decided to turn his back on the baseball diamond and hang out instead in the pool hall, defending his championship. There are varying versions of Kling's move from baseball to billiards. Either he was granted a leave of absence by the Cubs, even though he was already under contract, or he staged baseball's first recorded season-long holdout. In any event, the Cubs had to replace him, and their catching in 1909 was handled by Jimmy Archer and Pat Moran. Opponents noticed the difference.

After Johnny Kling and the Cubs parted ways before the 1909 season, both regretted the decision. Kling failed in his attempt to win another world billiards championship, and for the first time in four years, the Cubs failed to win the pennant. Kling's departure was the first chink in the armor of the Last Chicago Cubs Dynasty.

There were ominous signs for the Cubs early in the season, including an uncharacteristic five-game losing streak in the first week of May. Significantly, four of the losses came at home against Pittsburgh, and the sweep put the Pirates in first place. It was a spot they would never surrender. Honus Wagner put his personal exclamation mark on the sweep. In the second game of a May 2 doubleheader, he stole his way around the bases, swiping second, third, and finally home to account for a Pittsburgh run all by himself. And then, just to prove it was not an illusion, Wagner did the same thing the next day, leaving the Cubs rather dumbfounded. Wagner had just 29 other stolen bases that season, but he had made a statement to the Cubs in those two games. After finishing in second place in both 1907 and 1908, the Pirates were tired of chasing Chicago. They were not going away in 1909, and now the Cubs would have to chase them.

The Pirates moved into a handsome new ballpark in 1909. Triple-decked Forbes Field, named for a British general in the French and Indian War, was constructed of concrete and steel, the first stadium of its kind. The Cubs were in town for the stadium opener on June 30, 1909, and spoiled the Opening Day festivities by winning the game before a standing room–only crowd of 30,338.

The victory on the Opening Day of Forbes Field was part of a stretch of 10 wins in 14 games, the kind of dominant streak the Cubs were accustomed to running off in the previous three championship seasons. Those streaks would ordinarily give Chicago control of the pennant race; it did not work out that way this time. The Cubs simply couldn't shake the Pirates. Their win on Opening Day at Forbes Field left Chicago at a formidable 38–22, a comfortable 16 games over .500. The problem was the loss left the Pirates at 44–15, a more comfortable 29 games over the break-even mark and six and a half games ahead of the Cubs. Chicago posted an impressive 66–27 record the rest of the way. The problem for the Cubs was that the Pirates also went 66–27 following the May sweep.

Chicago's season-long pursuit of the Pirates was fueled by the Cubs' great pitching staff. "Three Finger" Brown won 27 games with a 1.31 earned run average. Ed Reulbach won 19 games including 14 in a row. Orval Overall was a 20-game winner with nine shutouts and led the league with 205 strikeouts. The staff ERA was a glittering 1.75, second lowest in history. They produced 32 shutouts, tying the record set by the White Sox in 1906.

And they finished in second place.

That's because the Pirates had assembled a potent offense that scored 699 runs. Led by Wagner, who won the batting title with a .339 average, the Pirates dominated the season's statistical charts. Wagner also led the league with 39 doubles and 100 runs batted in. Tommy Leach led the league with 126 runs scored and player-manager Fred Clarke was second with 97. By comparison, no Cubs hitter drove in more than 60 runs.

It's not as if the Cubs didn't try to wear down Pittsburgh. Chicago won 12 of 14 in July and had a 10-game winning streak in August. Over one stretch of September, the Cubs won seven of eight games. Over another stretch, they won eight of nine. It added up to 104 victories, five more than they managed when they won the pennant and World Series the year before. And it still left them six and a half games in back of Pittsburgh. No team has ever had a better record than the Cubs did that season and not won the pennant.

As the Pirates were closing in on the pennant, Charles Murphy, owner of the Cubs, tried to turn the tide of the season by reaching out to Washington and the president of the United States, William Howard Taft. Murphy's purchase of the Cubs in 1906 had been financed by the president's half-brother, and with the Cubs looking for any help they could get, the owner invited the president to set aside the affairs of state and spend a September afternoon at Chicago's West Side Grounds, watching the Cubs play the New York Giants.

Taft liked the idea. It was not unprecedented for a president to visit a ballpark. Benjamin Harrison had watched Cincinnati defeat Washington 7–4 on June 6, 1892. By all means, President Taft said, he would be happy to accept Murphy's invitation.

The president's arrival for the September 16 game was a riveting moment. Players from both teams lined up to greet President Taft and then, instead of sitting in a private reserved box, the president chose to sit among the fans. From there, he watched "Three Finger" Brown and Christy Mathewson stage another one of their epic battles, with the Giants prevailing 2–1. Did Taft enjoy the day? He must have. He stayed for all nine innings and was back for two more games in Pittsburgh and Chicago later that season. The following year, the president returned to Washington's National Stadium to throw out the first pitch opening the 1910 season, starting a presidential tradition that has become woven into the fabric of baseball, a uniquely American salute to the national pastime.

In all, President Taft attended 14 games while in office with stops in Pittsburgh, Chicago, St. Louis, and Cincinnati as well as Washington. He missed the 1912 season opener, though, because of the *Titanic* tragedy.

With Detroit winning the American League pennant, the 1909 World Series featured a showdown between two of baseball's biggest stars and opposing batting champions—the Pirates' Wagner and 22-year-old Ty Cobb of the Tigers. Cobb had batted .377 in 1909 with 107 runs batted in and 76 stolen bases.

Sam Crawford roamed the Tigers outfield alongside Cobb for 13 seasons and once offered this observation about his longtime teammate: "Cobb was a great ballplayer, no doubt about it. But he sure wasn't easy to get along with. He wasn't a friendly, good-natured guy like Wagner."[1]

Sometimes, though, Wagner wasn't good-natured. There is the oft-told tale, perhaps apocryphal, of an unpleasant episode at second base between the two players. Cobb liked to intimidate opponents. The story goes that he had Wagner in his crosshairs as he stood at first base and shouted at the Pirates shortstop.

"Watch out, Krauthead," Cobb is said to have yelled, channeling Wagner's German heritage. "I'm comin' down on the next pitch. I'll cut you to pieces."[2]

Wagner knew Cobb's reputation for hard-nosed baseball that often included sliding into bases with sharpened spikes in the air. Supposedly, the Pirates shortstop just grinned. He would be ready.

"Come ahead," Wagner is said to have shouted back.

According to legend, Cobb took off for second base as promised, and when he arrived there, Wagner had the ball waiting and tagged the runner in the mouth, splitting his lip and knocking out two teeth.

Cobb denied that it ever happened, but it was a good story and was widely repeated when the two men were inducted together in the first class at the Baseball Hall of Fame.

The World Series showdown between Wagner and Cobb never quite materialized. Wagner dominated in the Series, batting a robust .333 to Cobb's anemic .231. And he won the basepath battle, too, with six stolen bases to two for Cobb.

One of Cobb's steals was a missed call by umpire Silk O'Loughlin. The Pirates argued the safe call, but O'Loughlin was unmoved by their complaints. Finally, Cobb chimed in. "Of course, I was out," he said to the ump. "They had me by a foot. You just botched the play, so come on, let's play ball."

The battle between the Pirates and Tigers stretched to seven games, with Pittsburgh winning the last game 8–0. Wagner drove in two runs with a triple in the final game. Cobb went 0 for 4.

Watching all this were the Cubs, furious at the idea that the Pirates had knocked them off the National League throne they had so proudly occupied for three straight years. For the Pirates, it was one and done. They would not win another pennant until 1925. The Cubs, however, vowed that 1910 would be different for them. And it was.

The first part of their recovery was the return of their catcher. Johnny Kling had failed to defend the world billiards championship and decided to resume his baseball career. The Cubs, still annoyed at losing the 1909 pennant race to Pittsburgh, were not amused at Kling's season-long vacation and complained to baseball's National Commission about their vagabond catcher. Kling was fined $700, a substantial sum in those days, before he was allowed to return.

It turned out to be a small price to pay because, with Kling back, the Cubs set off on another 104-win season. Chicago made a statement early, going on an 11-game winning streak in late May to take command of the pennant race. The Cubs played with a chip on their shoulders, often pushing the envelope against opposing teams. Typical was a game in late June against Cincinnati when Joe Tinker became the first player to steal home twice in the same game.

The Cubs took over first place on May 24, and the turning point of the season may have occurred on July 11 when Franklin Adams authored his famous poem about the double-play combination of Tinker to Evers to Chance. Despite Adams's lyrical tribute, the trio never led the league in double plays, and there are people who insist that the catchy little rhyme went a long way to getting "the trio of bear Cubs" inducted into the Hall of Fame together in 1946.

The Cubs beat the Giants on July 11, the first of five straight losses and nine in twelve games for New York. The Giants trailed Chicago by just one and a half games when the tailspin started and were effectively done when it ended. Meanwhile, Pittsburgh dropped 9 of 11 at the end of May and could not get untracked after that. The Cubs lead had ballooned to 10 games over Pittsburgh and 12 over the New York Giants by the end of August.

Once again, the Cubs were fueled by their pitching staff, headed by "Three Finger" Brown, who won 25 games—his fifth straight 20-win season—and posted a 1.86 earned run average. As good as Brown was, his ERA was only second best in the league, trailing the 1.80 posted by a Cubs newcomer, Leonard "King" Cole, who had a 20–4 record and an .866 winning percentage, the best in franchise history. Included in his dazzling season was a no-hitter on July 31 when he beat St. Louis 4–0. The game was called after seven innings because both teams had to catch trains. Two other newcomers contributed, with Harry McIntyre, acquired from Brooklyn, winning 13 games and Lew Ritchie, who came over from Boston, adding 11.

Cole was a deliberate sort, and his slow play in poker games led manager Frank Chance to threaten him with a $50 fine if he didn't stop dawdling. After two seasons with the Cubs, Cole spent time with Pittsburgh and ended his career with the New York Yankees, where he had the distinction of surrendering the first Major League hit to a young Boston Red Sox player named Babe Ruth. Five years after his dazzling 1910 season, King Cole was dead at age 29 from tuberculosis.

The Cubs demonstrated some punch as baseball introduced a cork-centered baseball in order to inject more offense into the game. The Cubs responded with a league-leading 34 home runs including 10 by Wildfire Schulte, an almost unheard of total in the deadball days. They also led the league with 84 triples. Center fielder Solly Hofman batted .325, third best in the league, and led the team with 16 triples and 86 runs batted in.

Chicago clinched the pennant on October 2 at Cincinnati, punctuating the achievement by turning a triple play and finishing 13 games ahead of the New York Giants. But it was a Pyrrhic victory because, the day before the clincher, Johnny Evers broke his leg on a slide into home plate, casting a pall over the team. Evers did not let the injury keep him away from the World Series. Hobbling around on crutches, he spent time in the Cubs dugout during the World Series and kept up a steady stream of chatter directed at the umpires. His act was in stark contrast to the stately Philadelphia manager Connie Mack, who was in the other dugout.

Mack's young Philadelphia As finished a fat 14½ games in front of New York in the American League (AL), but even with the pennant runaway there was last-day drama in the AL involving the batting championship.

Ty Cobb, unpopular with the rest of the league, was battling Cleveland's Nap Lajoie for the batting title, and there was more than just glory at stake. The Chalmers Automobile Company announced that it would award a car to each league's leading hitter.

Cobb went into the final weekend leading the league with a .385 batting average, in position, it seemed, to claim the fancy Chalmers car. To protect his average, Cobb sat out the final two games. To catch him, Lajoie would need a fistful of hits on the last day. And that's what he got when St. Louis manager Jack O'Connor ordered third baseman Red Corriden to play deep every time Lajoie came to bat. The Cleveland star had eight hits in nine at-bats, six of them bunt singles.

The official averages gave Cobb the title by a fraction of a decimal point, and Chalmers, in a burst of good cheer, awarded cars to both players.

Meanwhile, the Cubs and Athletics were preparing for the World Series. Even without Johnny Evers, the Cubs were still favored against Mack's young A's, who had injury troubles of their own with outfielder Rube Oldring sidelined by a broken leg and ace pitcher Eddie Plank nursing a sore arm. But Mack had pitcher Jack Coombs, and he proved to be the difference.

Mack liked to cherry-pick talent from colleges and universities. His 1910 As were typical with first baseman Harry Davis from Girard College, second baseman Eddie Collins from Columbia University, shortstop Jack Barry from Holy Cross, and pitchers Chief Bender from Carlisle, Plank from Gettysburg College, and Coombs from Colby.

For the Series opener, Mack chose Bender, a 23-game winner, while Cubs manager Frank Chance went with Orval Overall. It proved to be a major mismatch. Bender took a one-hitter into the ninth inning and completed a three-hitter with eight strikeouts. Philadelphia knocked Overall out early with three runs and six hits in the first three innings. Frank Baker had three hits and two RBIs in the 4–1 victory.

For Game Two, Mack gave the ball to Coombs who, after four so-so seasons, had won 31 games and posted a 1.30 earned run average to anchor the A's pitching staff. The Cubs countered with Brown, and the duel between the two aces never really developed. Coombs, struggling all day with his control, gave up eight hits and nine walks, but the Cubs stranded 14 runners. Brown ran out of gas in the seventh inning when Philadelphia bunched four doubles and scored six runs on the way to a 9–3 victory.

After a day off for travel, Mack went right back to Coombs for Game Three against Chicago's Ed Reulbach. Both pitchers allowed a run in the first inning and two more in the second. Chance ran out of patience with Reulbach and went to his bullpen early. Philadelphia battered reliever Harry McIntyre for five runs in the third, three of them on a home run by Danny Murphy. But was it really a homer? Frank Chance didn't think so.

The Chicago manager argued that Murphy's ball should have been called a ground-rule double. The debate got rather heated as Chance aired out his well-known temper. The result was that he was thrown out of the game, the first umpire ejection in World Series history. It saved him from having to watch the A's 12–5 victory. Not only did Coombs go the distance, but also he contributed to Philadelphia's attack with three hits and three runs batted in.

Now, Mack's A's had a commanding 3–0 lead in the best-of-seven series and turned to Bender for the clincher against the Cubs' young King Cole. Murphy's fourth-inning double delivered two runs for Philadelphia, and the A's nursed a 3–2 lead into the ninth inning. Three outs away from elimination, the Cubs rallied.

Wildfire Schulte led off with a double, was sacrificed to third, and then scored on a triple by Chance. Chicago wasn't done yet. An inning later, the Cubs won the game when Jimmy Archer doubled with one out and scored on a two-out single by Jimmy Sheckard.

Brown had relieved Cole and thrown an inning in Game Four, but Chance went right back to him to start Game Five against Coombs, who had already won Games Two and Three for Philadelphia. The A's had a 2–1 lead after seven innings. Coombs led off the eighth with a single, igniting a five-run rally that sent the A's to a 7–2 victory.

Philadelphia had finished Chicago in five games, using just two pitchers—Coombs and Bender—to do the job. The A's were world champions, led to the title by Collins, who batted .429 and stole four bases. Baker batted .409 with nine hits, and Murphy batted .350 with nine runs batted in.

The A's had exposed the Cubs. Chicago was an aging team, and storm clouds were gathering over the franchise that had won four pennants and two world championships in five dominant seasons. Evers, who missed the Series when he broke his leg, then suffered a nervous breakdown that took him out of the lineup the next season. Chance was hospitalized with a blood clot in his head, played in just 31 games in 1911, and resigned a year later. Trades and retirements stripped the team of Kling, third baseman Harry Steinfeldt, Tinker, and Evers. Slowly, the team that had dominated the league was disappearing.

After the 1910 championship season, the Cubs would win just six more pennants and no World Series in a dry spell that has stretched over 100 years. There were great players and great moments to savor but no more championships. The Last Chicago Cubs Dynasty was history.

7

AND THEN...

The Last Chicago Cubs Dynasty ended with the 1910 World Series loss to Connie Mack's Philadelphia Athletics. That completed a five-year stretch during which the Cubs played .693 baseball, the highest percentage for any five-year period in the history of the sport. Chicago had dominated the first decade of 20th-century baseball, and now the run was over. One by one, the players drifted elsewhere, either to other teams or sometimes even to the new rival Federal League, and the Cubs began a downward spiral in the standings.

Some, like "Three Finger" Brown and Johnny Evers, returned to Chicago with new owner Charles Weeghman for encores after the Federal League fell apart. By then, though, the Cubs were afterthoughts in the National League, changing managers annually. Hank O'Day, the umpire in the middle of the Fred Merkle affair; Hall of Fame catcher Roger Bresnahan; and even old pal Joe Tinker each had a year as manager as the Cubs dipped in the standings. By 1917, the team had fallen to fifth place in its third straight losing season but still had a highlight moment—the only double no-hitter in baseball history.

The starting pitchers on May 2 were Jim "Hippo" Vaughn, a burly left-hander, for the Cubs and right-hander Fred Toney of the Cincinnati Reds. Vaughn was one of the Cubs' best pitchers, winning 20 or more games five times over a six-year period. Toney, who won 31 games in the previous two seasons and would win 24 that year, had spent parts of three seasons with the Cubs before joining the Reds. He also had once pitched a 17-inning no-hitter in the Bluegrass League, believed to be the longest no-hitter in organized baseball history. It was an interesting forerunner for what would occur on a cool, windy day before a small crowd of 3,000.

Vaughn sailed through the first nine Cincinnati batters before issuing a fourth inning walk to Heinie Groh, who was thrown out stealing. Then Gus Getz walked and was erased on a double play. Groh walked again later, and again the Cubs turned a double play. Rollie Zeider's error allowed Greasy Neale (later a prominent figure in the National Football League) to reach base, but he was caught stealing. Toney walked Cy Williams twice, in the second and fifth innings. Those were the only Cubs base runners through nine innings—an unprecedented double no-hitter.

Vaughn retired Gus Getz to open the 10th inning, but then Larry Kopf hit a grounder to the right of Cubs first baseman Fred Merkle—ironically, the same Fred Merkle whose baserunning mistake when he played for the Giants helped the Cubs down the stretch of the 1908 pennant race. Merkle, whose baseball odyssey had led him from the Giants through a brief stop in Brooklyn and then on to, of all places, the Cubs, dove for the ball, but it squirted past him for the game's first hit. Vaughn then retired Greasy Neale for the inning's second out. Hal Chase followed with a drive to right field that handcuffed Cy Williams for an error. Kopf stopped at third on the play. With Jim Thorpe, the Olympic hero who had won gold medals at the 1912 games in Stockholm, at bat, Chase stole second base.

Now, Vaughn was in a jam. He had handled Thorpe all day, striking him out twice. This time, Thorpe hit a high chopper in front of home plate. Realizing he would have a tough time catching the speedy Olympian at first base, Vaughn grabbed the ball and scooped it to catcher Art Wilson. Kopf, dashing home from third, arrived at the plate at the same time as the ball, which glanced off Wilson's chest protector. When Chase tried to score as well, Wilson recovered in time to tag him out. Thorpe, who spent six seasons in the majors but just one year with Cincinnati, was credited with a single on the play, and Toney took the slender one-run lead out to the mound for the bottom of the 10th.

Larry Doyle, leading off the inning, struck out. Then Merkle sent a long drive toward the left-field bleachers, but Cincinnati's Manuel Cueto ran to the wall to make the catch. That left Cy Williams standing between Toney and immortality. Williams worked the count to three and two and then struck out, completing Toney's no-hitter.

Cubs owner Charles Weeghman was outraged at his team being embarrassed by Toney and charged into the Chicago clubhouse to deliver a blistering, expletive-filled rant. Vaughn was less bothered by the turn of events, viewing it as just one more loss in what turned out to be a long season for him and the Cubs.

Things got better, however, in the very next year.

Before the 1918 season, the Cubs made two significant trades, acquiring pitchers Grover Cleveland Alexander from Philadelphia and Lefty Tyler from Boston. Alexander was coming off three straight 30-win seasons with Phillies, but with the United States entering World War 1, he found himself spending most of the season serving as a sergeant stationed in France with the 342nd Field Artillery. Alexander suffered partial hearing loss when a shell exploded near him, and that led to a seizure disorder that plagued him for the remainder of his Major League career. Tyler, however, became a much more significant addition to Chicago's staff.

With a reconfigured roster, the Cubs enjoyed a turnaround season, winning the National League pennant by 10½ games with an 84–45 record. With Alexander out of the picture, the pitching load was carried by Vaughn, who won the pitching Triple Crown, leading the league with 22 victories, 148 strikeouts, and a 1.74 earned run average while throwing 290⅓ innings. He had help from Tyler, who went 19–8 with a 2.00 ERA and 22 complete games, and Claude Hendrix, who was 20–7 with a 2.78 ERA and 21 complete games.

The war stripped many rosters of top players. The Boston Red Sox lost a fistful of stars but imported replacements like Stuffy McGinnis, Wally Shang, and Bullet Joe Bush. With left fielder Duffy Lewis off to the war, Boston used a young pitcher to replace him. Babe Ruth could hit as well as pitch, and he proved it, batting .300 and leading the league with 11 home runs. He also won 13 games as a pitcher, and he faced the Cubs and Vaughn in the opening game of the World Series.

Because of the war, the government imposed some restrictions on baseball, requiring the regular season to end by Labor Day and turning the World Series into a September instead of an October classic. The Series would also be limited to just one travel day. The Cubs drew the first three games at home and decided to play their home games in Comiskey Park, which was roomier than Weeghman Park (renamed Wrigley Field in 1926), with the remainder of the games ticketed for Boston.

In the Series opener, Vaughn again pitched a gem for Chicago but was the hard-luck loser. He allowed just one run on an RBI single by McGinnis in a fourth inning rally that included a single by veteran minor leaguer George Whiteman, but that was enough for Ruth, who pitched a six-hit shutout. In his autobiography, Ruth credited Whiteman, who platooned in left field with the Babe, especially against left-handers, with saving the shutout. First, Whiteman ran down Charlie Pick's bases-loaded drive for the final out of the first inning and then made another sparkling catch in the sixth with two runners on base. "They gave me credit for nine scoreless innings," Ruth wrote, "but this fellow Whiteman by his two great catches and his hit won the game three times over."[1]

The Cubs drew even in Game Two when Lefty Tyler beat Boston 3–1. Cubs manager Fred Mitchell thought left-handers had an edge against the Red Sox, so he brought Vaughn right back for Game Three. And again, Vaughn was a hard-luck loser, 2–1. This time, Whiteman robbed Dode Paskert of a fourth-inning home run. Red Sox starter Carl Mays retired the first two batters in the bottom of the ninth before Charlie Pick reached first base on an infield single. Pick then stole second and reached third on a passed ball. Now, Pick edged down the line and then took off, trying to steal home for the tying run. But Mays's pitch beat him, and Wally Schang tagged him out, ending the game.

Now the Series moved to Boston with t he Red Sox leading 2–1. Ruth was back on the mound for the Red Sox in Game Four and tripled home a pair of runs in the fourth inning against Tyler. That lead stood up until the eighth inning when the Cubs rallied for two runs, tying the score and ending Ruth's World Series scoreless streak at a record 29⅔ innings. But Boston regained the lead in the bottom of the eighth on a pinch single by Schang, a passed ball, and a throwing error by reliever Phil Douglas. When Chicago put the first two batters on base in the ninth, Guy Bush relieved Ruth and preserved the 3–2 victory for Boston.

There would be some drama that threatened the Series before Game Five. Attendance at Comiskey had been disappointing, under 28,000 for all three games. Baseball had already decided to include Series payouts to all first-division teams and to donate funds to war relief. That meant World Series shares for the Red Sox and Cubs would be reduced, a condition that did not please the players. There was talk of a strike before Game Five, and only an impassioned and lengthy plea from an inebriated American League president Ban Johnson prevented a walkout. Johnson appealed to the players' sense of wartime patriotism and saved the Series.

Down three games to one, Chicago sent Hippo Vaughn to the mound for Game Five, his third start of the Series. This time, Vaughn would emerge the winner, beating Boston's Sad Sam Jones 3–0 on a five-hitter. That left Vaughn with a 1–2 record for his three starts, even though he allowed just three runs and threw three complete games, a dominating display of pitching. The Series ended in Game Six with Carl Mays winning his second start 2–1 before a small Fenway Park crowd of just 15,238. Mays's 1.00 earned run average matched Vaughn's in a World Series in which just 19 runs were scored in six games.

The players' fears of reduced Series shares proved to be true. Each winning share was worth $1,108. Each losing share paid just $671.

Cubs manager Fred Mitchell had his fill of Phil Douglas, who had a continuing tendency to embrace alcohol, an affair that took him on occasional "vacations" from baseball. Fed up with that behavior, Mitchell demanded the Cubs unload Douglas, and they found a willing taker in the New York Giants. Manager John McGraw liked reforming players, and for a while, he succeeded in straightening out Douglas. It was only a temporary recovery though.

The year after Comiskey Park hosted the Cubs portion of the 1918 World Series, the White Sox won the American League pennant and the Series returned to the South Side of Chicago. This time, there was a cloud over the event with rumors of a fix everywhere. There were suspicions that Hal Chase and Lee Magee had done business with gamblers while they were with Cincinnati in 1918, and both were essentially blackballed from baseball. The chatter became louder in 1919 with talk that New York gambler Arnold Rothstein had conspired to arrange the outcome of the World Series games between the White Sox and Cincinnati. Eight Chicago players were implicated in the fix, and baseball staggered under the rumor that the game was on the precipice of a widespread scandal.

Then, there was the matter of Claude Hendrix.

Hendrix was a 20-game winner on the Cubs National League champions in 1918, one of the mainstays of the team's pitching rotation. By 1920, though, rumors of baseball fixes were everywhere, and Hendrix found himself in the middle of one of them. A flood of telegrams and phone calls reached the Cubs front office claiming that Hendrix had accepted money to throw a September start against Philadelphia. In response to the rumors, the Cubs made a last-minute pitching switch, starting Grover Cleveland Alexander. Alexander lost the game 3–0. An investigation followed, and Hendrix never pitched in the majors again. More importantly, a grand jury was convened to look into not only Hendrix's behavior but also the larger issue of baseball gambling and, of course, the 1919 World Series.

As the sport struggled to regain its footing following the Black Sox cloud, it became clear that major steps would have to be taken to restore the game's image. The first move was to hire a commissioner, and at the suggestion of Cubs stockholder A. D. Lasker, federal judge Kenesaw Mountain Landis got the job. He suspended the eight White Sox players for life and soon found former Cubs pitcher Phil Douglas on his doorstep.

Douglas had been somewhat productive for McGraw's Giants, but every so often his thirst for liquid refreshment again interfered with baseball. There were a number of drunken episodes, and after one of them, McGraw fined the pitcher $100 and suspended him without pay for five days. Peeved at the penalty, Douglas wrote a letter to outfielder Les Mann of the St. Louis Cardinals, offering to disappear for the rest of the season if the

Cardinals paid him off. The letter wound up on Landis's desk, and with baseball still reeling from the Black Sox affair, the commissioner acted swiftly. Within days, Douglas was suspended for life.

Meanwhile, following the 1918 World Series, the Cubs slipped back to mediocrity. For the next decade, they never finished higher than third, usually flirting with .500 records, losing as many games as they won, and going through a succession of managers. Fred Mitchell left after 1920, touching off a revolving door of bench bosses. He was followed by old pal Johnny Evers, whose sour disposition led to a series of clubhouse blow ups, including one that caused Hippo Vaughn to walk out in midseason. Bill Kellefer followed Evers for three full seasons and parts of two others. Then Rabbit Maranville took over for 50 games in 1925, a stretch pockmarked with his antics. His shenanigans did not amuse the Cubs bosses, and they quickly tired of his act. Next on the hot seat was George Gibson, who took over for the final weeks of the season. It all added up to a last-place finish, and Chicago brought in Joe McCarthy in 1926.

McCarthy had never played in the majors, and the Cubs job would be his first taste of the big leagues. He clashed with a number of players at the beginning and won a showdown with Alexander, demanding that the team unload the pitcher who was showing a greater affinity for drinking than he was for pitching. The Cubs began winning ball games, and McCarthy went on to assemble one of baseball's most successful managerial resumes. He became the first manager to win pennants in both leagues and posted career-winning percentages of .615 in the regular season and .698 in the World Series, both Major League records.

After finishing last in 1925, the Cubs recovered nicely under McCarthy, winning 82, 91, and 95 games in his first three years. In 1927, Jimmy Cooney was stationed at shortstop for a May 30 game against Pittsburgh. Cooney was a journeyman infielder, logging time with six teams over 11 years in a forgettable career. This day, however, would be memorable.

The Pirates, riding an 11-game winning streak, were leading 5–4 in the fourth inning when Lloyd Waner led off with a single. Clyde Barnhart walked, bringing Paul Waner, Lloyd's brother, to the plate. With the hit-and-run in place, Paul Waner drilled a line drive right at Cooney. The shortstop grabbed the ball and stepped on second to retire Lloyd Waner. Then he looked up to see Barnhart, who did not notice the catch, barreling toward second base. Cooney slapped the tag on the runner, completing an unassisted triple play, just the sixth one in modern Major League history.

It was a rare accomplishment, but the very next day, on May 31, first baseman Johnny Neun did the same thing for the Detroit Tigers. So maybe it wasn't so rare after all.

That same year, a second deck was added to Wrigley Field, and attendance soared past one million for the first time in franchise history. Things were looking up on the North Side of Chicago. The team was winning more games and moving up in the standings. And McCarthy was providing some stability in the dugout.

Meanwhile, the Cubs were also assembling a formidable roster that included future Hall of Famers Hack Wilson, Gabby Hartnett, Kiki Cuyler, and Rogers Hornsby. Wilson was drafted out of the Giants organization after frustrating John McGraw with his love for liquid refreshment. In 1929, Wilson led the league in runs batted in with 159 and was in the midst of leading the league in home runs four times in five years. Hartnett was drafted in 1922 and became a fixture behind home plate, the first catcher to hit 200 home runs and drive in 1,000 runs. Cuyler came over from Pittsburgh in exchange for third baseman Sparky Adams and outfielder Pete Scott. He led the league in stolen bases in his first three years with the Cubs, batted over .300 seven times in an eight-year stretch, and clinched the 1932 pennant for Chicago with a bases-loaded triple. Hornsby was the final piece of the puzzle, acquired from Boston before the 1929 season in exchange for five players and $200,000. He won seven batting championships, set a record with a .424 batting average in 1924, and had a career batting average of .358, second highest in history. In 1929, he batted .380, led the league with 156 runs scored, and was voted the National League's Most Valuable Player. Even without Hartnett, who sat out most of the season with an arm injury, the Cubs ran away with the National League pennant, winning the 1929 flag by 10½ games.

Waiting for them in the World Series once again were Connie Mack's Philadelphia Athletics. The A's were constructed slowly by Mack with sluggers like first baseman Jimmie Foxx, who supplied 33 home runs and batted .354; left fielder Al Simmons, who hit 34 home runs and batted .365; and catcher Mickey Cochrane, who hit .331, sprinkled through the lineup. The A's duplicated the Cubs' NL runaway, winning the American League pennant by 18 games over the second place New York Yankees. Mack's pitching staff was led by 24-game winner George Earnshaw and 20-game winner Lefty Grove. But the A's pulled a shocker in the Series opener, passing over their pitching mainstays and sending 35-year-old journeyman Howard Ehmke to the mound. Ehmke's claim to fame came six years earlier. Pitching for Boston, he threw a no-hitter against Philadelphia, a game in which Slim Harriss of the A's hit a ball off the wall but was declared out for missing first base. Ehmke followed that with a one-hitter against the New York Yankees.

Mack had nearly cut Ehmke from the team, but the pitcher pleaded for one more chance to pitch in the World Series and the manager relented. Mack excused Ehmke from the A's last road trip, keeping him behind in Philadelphia to scout the Cubs when they came to town to play the Phillies. Then the manager shocked the Cubs and his own team, sending Ehmke out to start Game

One of the Series before a crowd of 50,740 crammed into Wrigley Field. The veteran responded by striking out a record 13 batters in a 3–1 victory that made Mack look like a genius.

Earnshaw started Game Two for the A's, and Philadelphia charged to a 6–0 lead. But the Cubs rallied for three runs in the bottom of the fifth, and Grove came out of the bullpen to preserve the 9–3 victory. Once again, 13 Chicago batters struck out.

Now the Series moved to Philadelphia with the A's in command. After using Earnshaw for just 4⅔ innings in Game Two, Mack paraded his workhorse right back out to pitch Game Three for the A's. The Cubs needed a big game to get back in the Series, and they got one from Guy Bush, who scattered nine hits in a 3–1 victory. Chicago scored all its runs in the sixth inning in a rally that started when Bush drew a walk from Earnshaw.

The Cubs seemed poised to tie the Series when they charged out to an 8–0 lead in Game Four. Charlie Grimm homered, and Kiki Cuyler had three of Chicago's ten hits. Charlie Root was sailing along, throwing a three-hit shutout as the A's came to bat in the bottom of the seventh. And suddenly, things changed, thanks in large part to the late-afternoon sun that was peeking over the stands at Shibe Park. In center field, Chicago's Hack Wilson blinked at the glare. It had already caused him problems in the fifth inning when he lost a ball in the sun. Now it would lead to more trouble for him.

Al Simmons opened the inning with a home run. After Jimmie Foxx followed with a single, Bing Miller followed with a fly ball to center field. Wilson looked up, staggered a bit, and lost the ball, which fell for a single. Singles by Jimmy Dykes and Joe Boley made it 8–3, and Max Bishop followed with an RBI single. The 8–0 lead had been cut in half. Art Nehf relieved Root for the Cubs, and Mule Haas hit a fly ball to center field. Again, Wilson circled unsteadily and let the hit fall behind him, the second ball he lost in the sun in that inning. Haas circled the bases for a three-run homer, and the eight-run lead was all but gone. Mickey Cochrane walked and came around with the tying run on hits by Simmons and Foxx. After a hit batsman, Dykes doubled home two more runs, and the carnage was complete. Ten runs on 10 hits and two balls lost in the sun gave the A's a 10–8 lead. Lefty Grove retired the last six Chicago batters, four of them on strikeouts to seal the victory for Philadelphia.

The Cubs were all but done.

Embarrassed by the seldom-used Ehmke in the opener, they had blown an eight-run lead in Game Four. Chicago put up some resistance in Game Five, leading 2–0 into the ninth inning behind staff ace Pat Malone, who had won 22 games in the regular season. Then it all came apart. With one out, Bishop singled and Haas hit another home run, tying the score. Then doubles by Simmons and Miller brought home the winning run, and the A's were World Series champions again, and again at the expense of the Cubs. The sun had done in Wilson and his team.

It was not the only time Wilson experienced some adventures in the outfield. Years later, playing for Brooklyn, he was stationed in right field for another game at Philadelphia, where the wall had a tin facing. After a long night out, on a warm summer's afternoon, Wilson was resting quietly in the outfield, bent over with his hands on his knees, when manager Casey Stengel came to the mound to relieve pitcher Walter "Boom Boom" Beck. The pitcher, unhappy with the manager's decision, heaved the baseball into right field where it clanged off the tin facing. Awakened by the clatter, Wilson sprang into action, corralled the baseball, and relayed it to second base. "It was his best throw all season," Stengel said.

Wilson led the Cubs with eight hits and a .471 batting average in the Series, but his battles with the outfield sun, especially on Mule Haas's three-run homer, proved to be Chicago's undoing. A year later, Wilson went on an offensive tear, hitting .356, setting an NL record with 56 home runs and a Major League record with 191 runs batted in. Mark McGwire and Sammy Sosa later broke the home run mark, but for sustained hitting over the course of a season, Wilson's 1930 performance would be tough to beat.

Ownership was not pleased with the Cubs World Series failure against the As, and there was some tension between the front office and manager Joe McCarthy. Even though he had the team in a season-long pennant race against St. Louis in 1930, the hard feelings spilled over, and McCarthy was fired with four days left in the season and replaced by Rogers Hornsby. McCarthy wasn't out of work long, signing with the New York Yankees and going on to multiple pennants and world championships.

Hornsby's stewardship of the Cubs was not exactly serene. He clashed repeatedly with Hack Wilson, whose love of Chicago's nightlife did not sit well with the manager. Hornsby frowned on the slugger's continuing affair with alcohol. By the end of the 1931 season, the rift led to Wilson being traded away to St. Louis for pitcher Burleigh Grimes. Before that, however, catcher Gabby Hartnett shook things up at an exhibition game against the White Sox.

In early September at the urging of Mayor Anton Cermak, the Cubs and White Sox were scheduled to play an exhibition game at Comiskey Park to benefit Chicago's unemployed population. As the teams warmed up, a familiar character showed up in the field boxes. Mob boss Al Capone, awaiting his income tax evasion trial, had decided to take his son to a baseball game. Someone in Capone's party—it may have been the bootlegger himself—called out to Hartnett asking for an autograph. The catcher was happy to oblige, strolling over to the box seats, signing the ball, and having his picture taken. The photograph was splashed all over the country's newspapers, and Hartnett was soon called on the carpet by commissioner Landis, who frowned on the matter.

Hartnett had a classic defense for the judge. "I go to his place of business," the catcher said. "Why shouldn't he come to mine?"[2] Landis was not amused and issued an edict barring players and coaches from approaching spectators. Hartnett's retort was direct: "OK, if you don't want my picture taken with Al Capone," Hartnett said, "you go tell him."[3]

Ownership did not think the episode was funny, and with Hornsby's strict rules, the clubhouse was again a tense place. Then there was the manager's stunt of sending out a bench player to argue a call with the umpires instead of going out himself. The player was thrown out of the game, and a year later, Hornsby was gone, too. The Cubs finished with an 84–70 record, in third place, 17 games behind St. Louis in Hornsby's only full year as manager. When owner William Wrigley Sr. died before the start of the 1932 season, Hornsby's safety net was gone and, soon, so was the manager. Even though the Cubs were in second place, Hornsby was fired. Charlie Grimm, a more jovial character, took over as manager on August 2. The team responded, going 37–18 down the stretch to finish in first place.

How bad were the relations between Hornsby and his players? When the Cubs made it to the World Series, they did not vote a share of their postseason payoff to the ex-manager. Hornsby wasn't the only one who was shortchanged by the team that season. And that led to one of the most storied episodes in the history of baseball—Babe Ruth's "Called Shot" home run.

Billy Jurges was the Cubs shortstop in 1932 until July 6 when an ex-girlfriend, bent on suicide, confronted him in a hotel room. Armed with a pistol, she fired three shots, hitting Jurges twice. Suddenly, the Cubs found themselves with a gaping hole at shortstop. Their solution was to plug Mark Koenig in his place. Koenig had played for the 1927 Murderers Row New York Yankees but had drifted from New York to Detroit and then to the Pacific Coast League. With Jurges mending, the ex-Yankee became Chicago's shortstop and went on a tear, batting .353 in 33 games. The Yankees couldn't be happier for their old pal until they heard that the Cubs had given him the same treatment as they had to Hornsby when it came to voting World Series shares. Koenig actually did better than Hornsby. The infielder was voted a half share. The ex-manager was shut out completely. Koenig's old pals with the Yankees were outraged and let the Cubs know it when the two teams met in the 1932 World Series.

Leading the cacophony was old friend Babe Ruth. When the Cubs last encountered Ruth, he was a pitcher and beat them twice in the 1918 World Series. Now he had evolved into a larger-than-life slugger, who hit 60 home runs in 1927 and was the face of Major League baseball. In Joe McCarthy's second year as manager, the Yankees won the pennant by 13 games. As the World Series began, the Cubs' snub of Koenig held center stage.

The Series opened in New York, and the Yankees swept the first two games with plenty of bench jockeying going on between the two teams. Ruth was in the middle of the chatter, calling the Cubs "cheap chiselers," among other things. The Cubs gave it right back to the Babe when he butchered a couple of balls in the field and contributed little to the two Yankees victories. When they moved to Chicago for Game Three, the Babe uncorked a three-run homer in the first inning against Cubs starter Charlie Root. The score was tied at 4–4 when he came to bat again in the fifth inning. Root got ahead with a called strike and then missed with two pitches. Another called strike made the count two and two. On each pitch, Ruth raised his hand toward Root, as if to count "Strike one! Strike two!"

Now, with the Cubs bench riding him unmercifully, Ruth raised his bat and seemed to point to the centerfield bleachers. Or was he just motioning that he still had one strike left? On Root's next pitch, Ruth swung and connected for one of baseball's most legendary home runs—the Called Shot. Or was it? Could

Ruth have been so full of himself, so confident, that he would predict his home run? Root said, if Ruth had pulled a stunt like that, he would have knocked him down with the next pitch. Ruth skirted the argument, saying, "I didn't exactly point to any spot. . . . I just sort of waved to the whole fence, but that was foolish enough. All I wanted to do was give that thing a ride out of the park . . . anywhere."[4] Lou Gehrig followed Ruth's home run with one of his own, but it was lost in the hubbub over the "Called Shot."

The debate over Ruth's homer stretched well into the 21st century. There was no debate, however, over the Yankees' dominance of the Series. It was a four-game sweep for New York. Ruth had won the war of words in what turned out to be his last World Series, and Joe McCarthy had his revenge on the team that had fired him.

Now the Cubs began another revolving-door policy with their roster. Outfielder Babe Herman came from Cincinnati for four players and two years later was shipped to Pittsburgh. Pitcher Burleigh Grimes, acquired from St. Louis for Hack Wilson in 1931, was sent back to the Cardinals on waivers in 1933. That same year, Chuck Klein won the Triple Crown, leading the National League in batting, home runs, and runs batted in. Chicago packaged three players and $65,000 to get Klein, but he was a Cub for just two disappointing seasons before moving back to the Phillies in another trade. The Phillies also got first baseman Dolph Camilli from the Cubs.

Meanwhile, manager Charlie Grimm survived a series of scrapes with the front office, and by 1935, Chicago's revamped roster was back in contention. The holdovers were catcher Gabby Hartnett, who enjoyed a Most Valuable Player (MVP) season, batting .344 with 91 RBIs, and Billy Herman, Hornsby's replacement at second base, who hit .341 and led the league with 227 hits. Nineteen-year-old Phil Cavarretta moved in at first base, replacing player-manager Grimm, and drove in 82 runs. Billy Jurges had returned to shortstop, and Stan Hack was at third base. Outfielder Augie Galan, in his first full season, led the league in runs scored (133) and stolen bases (22). Twenty-game winners Bill Lee and Lon Warneke, later a National League umpire, anchored the pitching staff. The new-look Cubs went on an 11-game winning streak in late July. But after a so-so August in which they went 15–15, the Cubs surged to the league lead by winning 21 straight games through the month of September to finish four games in front of the defending champion St. Louis Cardinals Gashouse Gang. Chicago was back in the World Series.

This time, the Cubs would face the Detroit Tigers. The defending American League champions won their second straight pennant with a lineup built around slugger Hank Greenberg, catcher-manager Mickey Cochrane, second baseman Charlie Gehringer, and outfielder Goose Goslin. Schoolboy Rowe and Tommy Bridges were the mainstays of the Tigers pitching staff.

In the opener, Warneke outpitched Rowe, throwing a four-hitter in a 3–0 victory. Charlie Root, by now recovered from Babe Ruth's "Called Shot" home run, started Game Two for Chicago and was shelled. Jo-Jo White singled, Cochrane doubled, Gehringer singled, and Greenberg homered. The Tigers had a 4–0 lead, and Root was gone after four batters in what became an 8–3 Tigers victory. But it was a costly victory for Detroit. Greenberg, who hit 36 home runs and drove in 170 runs during the regular season, broke his wrist trying to score from first base in the seventh inning. He would be done for the Series.

The two teams moved to Chicago for Game Three. Trailing 3–1, the Tigers rallied for four runs in the eighth inning, two of them scoring on a single by Goose Goslin. But the 5–3 lead evaporated in the bottom of the ninth with the Cubs tying the score before Jo-Jo White's RBI single in the 11th gave Detroit a 6–5 victory. Alvin Crowder outpitched Tex Carleton in Game Four as

Detroit won 2–1, scoring the winning run on errors by Augie Galan and Billy Jurges. Now the Tigers were one win away from the World Series championship, but the Cubs held on. Lon Warneke threw six shutout innings, and Bill Lee finished up a 3–1 Chicago victory.

Back in Detroit for Game Six, the teams were tied at 3–3 in the top of the ninth inning. Stan Hack opened with a triple, putting Chicago in position to take the lead. Detroit pitcher Tommy Bridges was having none of that. He struck out Billy Jurges, got Larry French on a bouncer to the mound, and then retired Augie Galan on a fly ball, leaving Hack still standing on third base. Then the Tigers went about the business of finishing the Series. Mickey Cochrane singled with one out, moved to second on an infield out, and scored the winning run on Goose Goslin's single. The Tigers were world champions, and the Cubs had lost the World Series again.

Chicago was in a win-every-three-years pattern, reaching the World Series in 1929, 1932, and 1935, but losing the October classic each time. After losing to the Tigers in 1935, the team was in the chase the next two years, finishing second each season. Meanwhile, Wrigley Field was being spruced up with Bill Veeck planting ivy on the outfield walls in 1937 and the team adding a hand-operated scoreboard above the center field bleachers. Owner P. K. Wrigley also issued a directive, ordering announcers and broadcasters to never refer to Wrigley Field without using the adjective "beautiful" to describe the Cubs' home park. Wrigley also had one other foible. He believed baseball was meant to be played in the daytime. That's why, with all the upgrading he had done on the park, he never put in lights, and it was the absence of lights that led to one of the most memorable moments in the team's history.

The team struggled at the start of the 1938 season. When the Cubs lost nine of eleven in June, manager Charlie Grimm was on the hot seat. Even a six-game winning streak couldn't save him, and on July 20, he turned the team over to catcher Gabby Hartnett, who would double as player-manager. The team responded under Hartnett and staged a spirited chase after the Pittsburgh Pirates, who held first place for much of the season. By late September, the Pirates lead was down to one and a half games going into a crucial three-game series at Wrigley Field. Dizzy Dean, acquired from St. Louis for three players and $185,000 at the start of the season, beat Pittsburgh 2–1 in the opener, narrowing the Pirates' lead over the Cubs to one-half game. In the second game of the Series, Pittsburgh led 3–1 in the sixth, but Chicago rallied to tie the game. The same thing happened in the eighth with a Cubs rally tying the game at 5–5.

As darkness settled in over Wrigley Field, the umpires huddled and decided the game could continue for one more inning. If it were still tied after nine, the teams would play a doubleheader the next day. Pittsburgh reliever Mace Brown retired the first two hitters in the bottom of the ninth, bringing up Hartnett. The player-manager swung and missed at the first pitch and fouled off the next one. Then Brown hung a curve ball. "I had just one swing left," Hartnett said. "Brown pumped with everything he had and I swung with every ounce of strength I possessed. I've heard that some people didn't think the ball would carry into the bleachers. I never had that fear. I felt it was gone the very second I hit it."[5]

Baseball had not yet come up with the catchphrase "walkoff homer," but Hartnett had delivered a big one for the Cubs. He was mobbed by fans and teammates as he rounded the bases with his game-winning shot. It became known as "the homer in the gloamin,'" playing off a popular 1911 tune "Roamin' in the Gloamin,'" with *gloamin'* being a regional dialect term for twilight. Now the Cubs were in first place, and they solidified that standing with a 10–1 victory the next day, completing the sweep of the

Pirates. It was Chicago's 10th straight victory, and three days later, the Cubs clinched the pennant.

Chicago's prize for the dramatic championship was a World Series date with the New York Yankees, who were in the midst of winning seven American League pennants in eight years. The Yankees had swept the Cubs in the 1932 Series, punctuated by Babe Ruth's "Called Shot" home run. By now, Ruth had signed on as trophy coach for the Brooklyn Dodgers, but it made little difference to New York's offense.

The Yankee lineup was loaded with big bats like Joe DiMaggio, Lou Gehrig, Bill Dickey, Joe Gordon, and Tommy Henrich. Each of them had at least 22 home runs and 90 runs batted in during the regular season, and all except Henrich were headed for the Hall of Fame. Facing them was a daunting challenge for opposing pitching staffs.

In the opening game of the Series, Dickey went four for four, driving in one run and scoring another as Red Ruffing outpitched Bill Lee. The Cubs sent Dizzy Dean out against Lefty Gomez in Game Two. But this was not the vintage Dean, who once dominated batters for the St. Louis Cardinals Gashouse Gang. This was a different Dean. Using an altered delivery after suffering a broken toe in the 1937 All-Star Game, he had hurt his arm. The Cubs had picked him up in April, and he went 7–1 for them in 13 games. Against the Yankees, he used an assortment of pitches to hold them to just three hits, and the Cubs led 3–2 after seven innings. In the eighth inning, Frankie Crosetti, perhaps the least likely Yankee long-ball threat after hitting just nine in the regular season, tagged Dean for a two-out, two-run homer to give New York a 4–3 lead. Then in the ninth, DiMaggio hit another two-run shot, and the Yankees had a 6–3 victory.

Now the Series moved to New York with the Cubs on the ropes. Dickey and Gordon homered in New York's 5–2 victory in Game Three, and the Yankees completed the sweep with an 8–3 victory in Game Four. Crosetti, the Game Two hero, added a double and triple and four more RBIs. It was a one-sided Series victory for New York, the Yankees' third straight world championship. But it came with an ominous note. Gehrig went just 4 for 14, all singles. Early next season, the strapping first baseman's consecutive game streak ended at 2,130, and two years after that, he would be dead from a rare degenerative disease, amyotrophic lateral sclerosis.

In the wake of being swept away in four straight games by the Yankees, the Cubs applied a shakewell solution to their roster. Billy Herman and Larry French were shipped to Brooklyn in separate trades. Billy Jurges was dealt to the New York Giants in a six-player swap that delivered shortstop Dick Bartell. Then, exactly one year after acquiring Bartell, the Cubs shipped him to Detroit for Billy Rogell. First baseman Babe Dahlgren was purchased from Boston on June 15, 1941, and then sold to Brooklyn on May 19, 1942. Pitcher Hank Gornicki was purchased from the Cardinals on September 2, 1941, and then sold to Pittsburgh three months later. Pitcher Lon Warneke, traded to the Cardinals in 1936, returned to Chicago in 1942. First baseman Jimmie Foxx, nearing the end of a Hall of Fame career, came over from the Boston Red Sox in 1942, and pitcher Paul Derringer was acquired from Cincinnati in 1943.

The flurry of trades created a rotating roster but not much progress in the standings. After finishing in fourth place in 1939, the Cubs endured five straight losing seasons for the first time in franchise history. Hartnett left as manager after the 1940 season, replaced by Jimmie Wilson, who made it into 1944. But 13 losses at the start of that season doomed him, and old friend Charlie Grimm came back to the dugout for a second stint as manager.

With World War II sapping big league rosters, owner P. K. Wrigley, always an innovator, created the All American Girls Professional Baseball League in 1943. The female players, immortalized by Hollywood in the film *A League of Their Own*, played for the Rockford (Illinois) Peaches, the Chicago Colleens, the Fort Wayne Daisies, and the Kalamazoo Lassies; the league stayed in business until 1954. Among the managers were Hall of Famers Jimmie Foxx and Max Carey.

Meanwhile, the Cubs roster remake eventually paid dividends, and by 1945, Chicago was back in the World Series. Phil Cavarretta was the National League's Most Valuable Player, leading the league with a .355 batting average. He drove in 97 runs and scored 94. Center fielder Andy Pafko finished second in the MVP balloting with 110 RBIs. Peanuts Lowrey returned from World War II service and batted .283 with 89 RBIs. But the most important acquisition came in late July when the Cubs paid the New York Yankees $97,000 for pitcher Hank Borowy.

Borowy had been the Yankees' best pitcher, winner of 10 games up until that point. But a bit of a midseason slump convinced management to put him on waivers, making him available for the bargain price of $7,500. Other teams thought the Yankees would pull him back if Borowy was claimed and passed on him. Now, they had waivers on him, and when the Cubs inquired, the Yankees made the deal, earning the team considerably more than the waiver price for the pitcher. The rest of the American League teams were outraged, believing they had been tricked by New York. It wasn't the first time and it wouldn't be the last that the Yankees were despised by their AL partners.

The Cubs pitching staff was anchored by Hank Wyse, who won 22 games, and Claude Passau, who added 17. But they were both right-handers, and Borowy was a left-hander, balancing out the rotation. He had gone 10–5 in New York but really blossomed with the Cubs, going 11–2 and leading the National League with a 2.13 earned run average. He also became manager Charlie Grimm's go-to guy and showed why in the opening game of the World Series against the Detroit Tigers. Ten years earlier, the

Tigers had defeated the Cubs in six games. This time, Chicago was determined to get even, especially when, with hotel space in short supply in Detroit, the team was housed in two steamships with the players squeezed into tiny staterooms.

In the opener, the Cubs shelled 25-game winner Hal Newhouser for seven runs in the first three innings on their way to a 9–0 romp. Bill "Swish" Nicholson drove in three runs with a single and a triple, and Borowy scattered six hits for the victory. Detroit went with Virgil "Fire" Trucks in Game Two, an interesting choice since the Tigers had 18-game winner Dizzy Trout available. Trucks had just been discharged from the service and made only one start before the Series, throwing five innings on the final day of the regular season as the Tigers clinched the pennant on Hank Greenberg's ninth-inning grand-slam home run against the defending champion St. Louis Browns. Trucks responded with a seven-hitter, and Greenberg supplied a three-run homer for a 4–1 Detroit victory.

In Game Three, Claude Passau returned to Detroit's Briggs Stadium for the first time since the 1941 All-Star Game when Ted Williams tagged him for a two-out, three-run home run in the ninth inning that gave the American League a 7–5 victory. This time, Passau threw a one-hitter for the Cubs, allowing only a second-inning single by Rudy York in a 3–0 victory. It was just the second one-hitter in Series history, joining the Cubs' Ed Reulbach, who did it to the White Sox in 1906. Since then, there have been two other World Series one-hitters—Bill Bevans of the Yankees in 1947, who lost a no-hitter in the ninth inning against Brooklyn, and Jim Lonborg of the Red Sox in 1967 against the St. Louis Cardinals.

The 1945 Series moved to Chicago for Game Four, and Ray Prim retired the first 10 Tigers he faced. Then it all came apart. Roy Cullenbine drove in two runs with a double in the fourth inning, and Detroit won 4–1 on Trout's five-hitter. Now, with the

Series tied at two games apiece, Charlie Grimm went right back to Hank Borowy, who had become the Cubs meal ticket. The Tigers started Newhouser, who had been blasted in Game One. This time, the Tigers ganged up on Borowy for four straight hits in the sixth inning, breaking open a 1–1 game with four runs as Newhouser went the distance in an 8–4 victory.

On the brink of losing the Series, the Cubs gave the ball to Passau for Game Six with Trucks starting for the Tigers. Stan Hack's bases-loaded single keyed a four-run Chicago rally in the fifth inning, and the Cubs led 5–1 in the seventh. Then a line drive caught Passau in his pitching hand, tearing the nail off his middle finger, and he was forced to leave the game. The Tigers rallied against the Chicago bullpen and tied the score at 7–7 on an eighth-inning home run by Greenberg. As the game stretched into extra innings, it settled into a battle between Borowy and Trout, both working in relief. Borowy threw four hitless innings, and the Cubs pushed across the winning run in the 12th inning when Hack's hit bounced off a sprinkler head in left field allowing the winning run to score. The Series would be settled in a seventh game.

After a day off, Grimm went right back to Borowy, who had thrown four innings in Game Six and five innings in Game Five following his complete game in the Series opener. The Cubs meal ticket had nothing left. He allowed singles to the first three Detroit batters and was yanked for Paul Derringer. By the time the Tigers were done, they had five runs before the Cubs came to bat. That was plenty for Newhouser, who went the distance for a 9–3 victory.

Once again, for the sixth time since the Last Chicago Cubs Dynasty ended, the team had lost a World Series. This one, however, was more significant because it was last time in the 20th century and the last time in 70 years that they played in one. The last surviving player from that team was infielder Lenny Merullo.

In 2014, he was invited back to throw out the first pitch at a game during the 100th anniversary of Wrigley Field. He died a year later at age 98.

8

CURSES, CATS, AND OTHER CALAMITIES

There are times when followers of the Chicago Cubs—fans, players, and executives—will swear this team needs an exorcism, a complete cleansing of the soul from the curses and other unfortunate conditions that have dogged this franchise over the years.

If it wasn't Babe Ruth calling his shot against them, it was a billy goat barred from entry at Wrigley Field and its owner cursing the team in perpetuity. If it wasn't a committee of coaches appointed to run the team in a sort of managerial merry-go-round, it was a poor innocent fan, reaching out of the stands for a foul ball and touching off another tragedy in 2003. The Cubs scored 22 runs against Philadelphia on May 17, 1979, ordinarily more than enough to secure a win or maybe two or three. The problem was that day the Phillies scored 23.

Black cats dashing in front of the dugout. Unfortunate trades. It's always something. When they installed lights at Wrigley in 1988 so that they could add night games to a previously all-day schedule, the first game was rained out. Some thought it was a message from God not to disturb the last outpost for day baseball.

There is good reason that the Cubs fan club was named the Emil Verban Society, honoring the memory of an otherwise forgettable infielder whose mediocre play sort of epitomizes the history of the franchise. The membership list of over 700 included some high-profile folks like Hillary Rodham Clinton, Bill Murray, and Bryant Gumbel. Even Barack Obama, an ardent White Sox fan, was added as a sort of prank by the Verban Society membership. They are all accustomed to the frustration of the Cubs.

It is a fact that since the blessed season of 1945—Chicago's last National League championship year—31 different Major League franchises have been to the World Series, none of them named the Cubs. And it seems as if everyone, even the much-pitied Boston Red Sox, has won the World Series—three, in fact, for the Red Sox—since the last time the Cubs managed that trick during the Roosevelt administration—Theodore, not Franklin.

The hard times are well past a hundred years now. The Cubs last ruled baseball in 1908, a time when horseless carriages and handlebar mustaches dotted the American landscape. They invented radio after that. Television, too. Harry Caray, Cubs broadcaster of blessed memory, was born after that year. And died, too.

Arizona, New Mexico, Alaska, and Hawaii were added to the union. Prohibition came and went. Twelve amendments were added to the Constitution, and America elected 18 presidents, some of them more than once, all after that.

The NBA, NHL, and NFL were all formed, and Chicago teams won championships in each of those leagues. None of the success rubbed off on the Cubs though.

Hall of Famer Ernie Banks labored through 19 champion-less seasons with the Cubs but maintained his optimism. "You've got to be patient," he once explained. "It takes time. These things don't happen overnight."

One day, during the depths of the baseball depression on the North Side of Chicago, Hall of Fame announcer Jack Brickhouse tried to explain away the trials and tribulations of the Cubbies, observing, "Well, any team can have a bad century."

Indeed.

For proof of that, consider that since winning the 1908 World Series, the Cubs have finished in last place 16 times and have finished at least 30 games behind in the standings 15 times. A variety of Cubs pitchers have struggled through eight 20-loss seasons. The team has lost seven World Series and been swept in three division playoff series and the 2015 League Championship Series.

It has been a distressing litany of despair, but it was not always thus. In the early years of the 20th century, the Cubbies were the best team in baseball, a veritable juggernaut that won three straight pennants and four in five years. There were consecutive World Series titles, a heady time in the Second City. It was a time when the Cubs ruled baseball, and no one could have imagined the roller coaster adventures that were ahead for this grand old franchise.

There was a time after their dynasty years when the Cubs were not awful. Starting in 1929, the team reached the World Series with some regularity—1932, 1935, 1938, and finally, 1945. And then came the Curse.

The World Series that year began in Detroit, and Chicago won two of the first three games behind the strong pitching of Hank Borowy and Claude Passau. Now they were coming home to Wrigley Field, and the fans were energized. Particularly excited was local saloonkeeper Billy Sianis, who invested $7.20 to purchase a pair of tickets for Game Four. One ticket was for Sianis. The other was for his bar's mascot, a goat named Murphy.

There was some disagreement at the Wrigley gate, where Sianis was told that animals were not permitted in the ballpark. Eventually, that was resolved—after all, Sianis argued, Murphy had a ticket—and the pair were permitted to walk around the field during pregame practice with Murphy wearing a placard that said, "We got Detroit's Goat." Soon, however, word came from the front office. Murphy had to go. Sianis asked why, and he was told, "Because the goat stinks."

Sianis was properly outraged. After all, $7.20 was no small piece of change in 1945. He and Murphy left the ballpark but not before making an announcement. "The Cubs ain't gonna win no more. There ain't gonna be no more World Series in Wrigley Field."[1]

Nobody took the proclamation from the angry saloonkeeper very seriously, until Detroit won three of the next four games to capture the World Series. It was then that Billy Sianis fired off a telegram to Cubs owner P. K. Wrigley. It contained just three words: "Who stinks now?" Murphy the goat lived another 20 years. Only once over that period did the Cubs finish higher than fifth.

There have been efforts through the years to relieve the Cubs from the burden of the Curse. Perhaps believing the Cubs had suffered long enough, Billy Sianis announced in 1979 that he was rescinding the Curse. The team finished fifth again. Five other times, goats have been ushered onto Wrigley Field. Once Ernie Banks, perhaps the franchise's most beloved player, was convinced to lead one of the animals around the infield. It was to no avail. Long after Billy Sianis and Murphy passed away, the Curse remained.

And then, it seemed to morph into other mysterious incarnations. In 1969, the Cubs seemed headed for the postseason, ending almost a quarter century of frustration. They led the National League's Eastern Division for 155 days, riding strong performances by pitcher Ferguson Jenkins, third baseman Ron Santo, and first baseman Ernie Banks, all headed for the Hall of Fame. Their major competition came from an unlikely source, the expansion New York Mets, who had never experienced any success in the previous seven years of their existence. The Cubs lead was nine games in August, and it seemed as if they would win the division easily. But the Mets just wouldn't go away.

By the time Chicago came to New York for a crucial series in September, the Mets had crept to within one and a half games of the Cubs. In the first inning of the series opener on September 8, Santo was on deck when a small cat appeared from under the stands and went for a leisurely stroll in front of the Chicago dugout. This was not just any old cat though. This was a black cat, part of a colony of feral cats who made Shea Stadium their home.

A black cat!

Santo stared at the feline with some understandable apprehension. "I knew right away we were in trouble," the third baseman said later. "I wanted to run and hide."[2] The Miracle Mets went on to sweep the Series to move into first place. They then won the pennant and the World Series and left the Cubs and their fans wondering about curses and cats.

P. K. Wrigley was never a stand-still owner. He always sought ways to improve the Cubs and often came up with innovative ideas. They didn't always work, but he was not shy about trying new things. There was, for example, the case of the College of Coaches.[3]

Tired of hiring and firing managers one after another, Wrigley decided on a different approach in 1961. Instead of one manager calling the shots, the Cubs dugout would use a committee approach. There would be relief managers, just like relief pitchers. Originally, eight coaches were appointed: Bobby Adams, Rip Collins, Harry Craft, Charlie Grimm, Vedie Himsl, Goldie Holt, Elvin Tappe, and Verlon Walker. Seven had ties to the Cubs organization, most prominently Grimm, who had managed the team three different times. Holt came over from the Los Angeles Dodgers, where he had served as a roving pitching instructor.

Four coaches took turns as head coach in 1961. Together, the new brain trust led Chicago to a seventh-place finish with 64 wins, just four more than the Cubs had managed the year before when Lou Boudreau and Grimm shared the manager's seat. Wrigley was not deterred. He added three more coaches—Lou Klein, Fred Martin, and Charlie Metro—to the rotation for 1962, resulting in 59 wins (the fewest in modern team history) and a ninth-place finish. The only team to finish behind the Cubs that year was the woeful expansion New York Mets, who lost a record 120 games.

Bob Kennedy was appointed head coach for the full season in 1963, and the team finished 82–80, its first winning season since 1946. That earned Kennedy another year as head coach, and in 1964, the college added an athletic director, retired air force officer Robert V. Whitlow, who liked to work out before games, suiting up with uniform No. 1, just in case there was any confusion over who was in charge.

Kennedy won more games (182) than any of the other head coaches but was notified between games of a 1965 doubleheader against Cincinnati that it was Klein's turn to be head coach. That kind of perpetual confusion left the team floundering. After five seasons, the Cubs scrapped Wrigley's college concept with an overall record of 353–449. Perhaps the most notable event during the college's reign was Chicago's trade of outfielder Lou Brock to St. Louis in exchange for pitcher Ernie Broglio. Brock had a Hall of Fame career with the Cardinals while Broglio won seven games in three years with the Cubs. It is not clear which coach signed off on that deal.

When P. K. Wrigley died in 1977, control of the team passed to his son, William, who declared the Cubs were not for sale. Four years later, young Wrigley sold his 81 percent of the team to the Chicago Tribune Company. The new owners brought in ex–big league pitcher and manager Dallas Green to run the team, and by 1984, the Cubs were division champions, back on top for the first time since 1945. Green had traded for pitcher Rick Sut-

cliffe, who went 16–1 to win the Cy Young Award. Second baseman Ryne Sandberg was the MVP, batting .314 with 19 home
runs. Two of the homers came in the ninth and tenth innings of a
June game against St. Louis, keeping the Cubs alive for a 12–11
victory. Clearly there was some magic going on at Wrigley Field.

And then came the playoffs.

Chicago won the first two games at home and needed just one
more win in San Diego to advance to the World Series. This
would be no small achievement, considering the nearly 40-year
postseason dry spell. But the Padres would not go quietly, coming
from behind to win Game Three and Game Four. Now it would
all come down to a decisive fifth game. In the dugout, minutes
before Game Five, Sandberg was thirsty and reached for some
Gatorade. The liquid spilled all over first baseman Leon Durham's glove, soaking it. Now, with the first pitch just minutes
away, Durham frantically toweled off the glove and even employed a hair dryer.

The Cubs were leading 3–2 in the seventh inning when Tim
Flannery sent a squibbler toward first base. Durham reached for
it with his glove, which by then had dried in the California heat.
The ball slid by for a crucial error. The Padres rallied for a 6–3
victory and advanced to the World Series. Once again, the Cubs
went home. Was Durham's Gatorade-soaked glove the reason?
The first baseman never said that, but he did note, "That's kind of
eerie."

It took a while for the Cubs to recover from that shock. There
were cameo postseason berths in 1989 and 1998, but by 2003,
Chicago seemed on the path to putting all the disappointments
behind. That was the year that the Cubs won a postseason series
for the first time since winning the 1908 World Series. Chicago
eliminated Atlanta in the first round in 2003, moving on to face
the Florida Marlins. Chicago led the best-of-seven National
League Championship Series three games to one. Just one more

win and the Cubs would be back in the World Series for the first time since 1945.

Florida won Game Five on a two-hitter by Josh Beckett, but there was no panic by the Cubs. They were going home. The remainder of the Series would be played in the friendly confines of Wrigley Field. Besides, Chicago had one of its aces, 18-game winner Mark Prior, who won Game Two, primed for the start.

What could go wrong?

Plenty.

The Cubs were leading 3–0 with one out in the eighth inning of Game Six. World Series plans were in the works with Chicago just five outs away from the Fall Classic and Prior in complete control, working on a three-hit shutout. He got Luis Castillo to lift a lazy fly ball in foul territory down the left-field line. Left fielder Moises Alou closed in on the ball, seeming ready to make the catch. And then, disaster!

Several fans reached for the ball. One was 26-year-old Steve Bartman, wearing glasses, a Cubs hat, and earphones. As Alou jumped, Bartman reached out and deflected the ball. It fell into the stands untouched. An outraged Alou reacted angrily, slamming his glove to the ground and shouting at the fans. Castillo had another life and walked. Suddenly, it all fell apart on the Cubs.

In what seemed like a heartbeat, the Marlins sent 12 men to the plate and rallied for eight runs. There was a key error by usually sure-handed shortstop Alex Gonzalez and a bases-loaded double by light-hitting Mike Mordecai that broke the game open. Bartman became the villain. Suddenly, the friendly confines of Wrigley Field were not so friendly. Fans cursed and threw debris at him as he was ushered out of the ballpark by security guards. The Marlins overcame a 5–3 deficit the next day for a 9–6 victory and went on to defeat the New York Yankees in the World Series.

Bartman was under siege and released a statement to try and calm the waters, saying, "From the bottom of this Cubs fan's heart, I am truly sorry." The Bartman Ball was sold at auction for $113,000 the next year and then demolished in a ceremony at Harry Caray's restaurant before the start of the 2004 season. It was viewed as a sort of exorcism to remove any bad karma remaining from the episode. The fact is, however, that Bartman has not returned to Wrigley Field, and the Cubs did not win a postseason game from then until the 2015 divisional playoffs.

9

AFTER THE DYNASTY

Nothing lasts forever, and that included the Last Chicago Cubs Dynasty, which fell victim to age, illness, desertion, and greed and dissolved piece by piece following its domination of the National League in the first decade of the 20th century.

The Cubs had baseball's deepest pitching staff, led by Mordecai "Three Finger" Brown. But when the dynasty began to dissolve, even the best pitching staff in baseball couldn't preserve it.

Consider that Chicago's most frequent lineup in 1911 as defending National League champions had the obscure Vic Saier at first base instead of Frank Chance, Jimmy Archer catching instead of Johnny Kling, Heinie Zimmerman at second base instead of Johnny Evers, and Jimmy Doyle at third base instead of Harry Steinfeldt. It was a vastly different looking team.

The shabby performance of the Cubs in the 1910 World Series against Philadelphia was uncharacteristic and suggested that perhaps the team was simply getting old. Management was not going to stand idly by and watch that happen. Kling and Steinfeldt were traded away. Injuries kept Evers and Chance on the sidelines. Sometimes, though, management had nothing to say about the different look of the roster.

Orval Overall walked away by himself, retiring at age 29.

Overall was the No. 3 pitcher on the Cubs staff behind Brown and Ed Reulbach but battled periodic arm trouble. He began his career with Cincinnati going 18–23 and carrying a heavy workload of 318 innings in 42 appearances in 1905. When he got off to a poor start in 1906, the Reds sent him to the Cubs.

Frank Chance believed Overall's arm problems were related to his workload and used him less frequently. Overall prospered, going 12–3 with a 1.88 earned run average as the Cubs won 116 games. The next year, the big Californian won 23 games.

Overall strung together 14 consecutive victories from August 11, 1907, through May 12, 1908. The next year, Overall enjoyed his best season, going 20–11 and leading the league with nine shutouts and 205 strikeouts. His ERA was 1.42, best of his career and third best in the National League that season.

Even though they won 104 games, the Cubs missed the World Series in 1909. When they returned to the Series with another 104 wins in 1910, Overall's arm problems limited him again. He went 12–6 with a 2.68 ERA but earned the Game One start in the World Series against Philadelphia. Knocked out in three innings, he never regained his form. After a contract dispute with the Cubs, he returned to California to work in a gold mine he owned with teammate "Three Finger" Brown. He stayed in shape by playing some semipro ball and even attempted a comeback with the Cubs in 1913 when he went 4–5.

After leaving baseball, Overall went into the banking business and even ran unsuccessfully for Congress. He died of a heart attack at age 66 on July 14, 1947.

The Cubs also lost Overall's catcher in 1911. Although he was not as celebrated as some of his teammates, Johnny Kling was viewed as the glue that held the Cubs together. When he left the team to play billiards in 1909, Chicago's string of three straight National League pennants ended. When he returned a year later, the Cubs finished first again. It was not a coincidence.

Kling was a defensive star, and from 1902 to 1908, he led National League catchers in putouts six times. But in the 1910 World Series, Kling, a career .272 hitter, batted just .077. He was also 36 years old and had angered management with his absence in 1909. He also got off to a bad start in 1911, batting just .175 in 27 games. In June he was shipped off to Boston in an eight-player trade. He struggled through the worst season of his career, batting just .224.

A year later, the franchise was sold, and Kling was appointed manager, replacing Fred Tenney. Kling enjoyed a renaissance at the plate, batting a career-best .317 in 81 games. But the team finished in last place, and Kling's managerial career was over. He was shipped to Cincinnati where he played one more season before retiring.

After leaving baseball, Kling returned to Kansas City where he worked in real estate. In the basement of a local hotel, he opened the Pennant Café, complete with a billiards room with chandeliers made of bats and balls and four baseball-themed sidewalk windows, one for each of the Cubs pennants. For two years, Kling owned the Kansas City Blues of the American Association. In 1937, he sold the team to Jacob Ruppert of the New York Yankees, and it became the Yankees primary farm club.

Steinfeldt had been the final piece of the Tinker-to-Evers-to-Chance infield and had five productive seasons as the Cubs third baseman. But it took him some time to get there.

In the early 1890s, Steinfeldt toured the country with a minstrel show, playing baseball in whatever town the show was booked. He turned to baseball full time in 1895 and three years later reached the Major Leagues with Cincinnati. When the team released Charlie Irwin in 1901, Steinfeldt became the Reds regular third baseman. In 1903, he batted .312 and led the National League with 32 doubles.

By 1905, however, the Reds decided to part ways with Steinfeldt and traded him to Chicago for infielder Hans Lobert and pitcher Jake Weimer. Cubs manager Frank Chance plugged Steinfeldt in at third base, completing the Cubs' most famous infield. Steinfeldt responded with the best season of his career, batting .327 and leading the league with 176 hits and 83 runs batted in as Chicago won a record 116 games. A year later, he led the Cubs to their World Series championship against Detroit when he batted .471.

After that, however, Steinfeldt's production began to fall off. He batted just .241 in 1908 and then .252 in each of the next two seasons. After going just 2 for 20 in the 1910 World Series and then holding out for a new contract, the team soured on him. He was put on waivers and sold to St. Paul of the American Association. Early in the 1911 season, he was acquired by Boston, where he joined old pal Johnny Kling. But by July, he came down with a serious illness. After recovering, he briefly managed Cincinnati of the United States League, and after that circuit folded, he tried out with the Cardinals before being cut.

There were brief stops in Louisville, Chattanooga, and Meridan, but he was still feeling the effects of his illness. He returned home and died on August 17, 1914, of a cerebral hemorrhage. He was just 37 years old.

The Cubs replaced Steinfeldt at third base with Jimmy Doyle, who also came over from Cincinnati. But the franchise was jolted when, after just one season, Doyle suffered an appendicitis attack and died.

With Overall, Kling, and Steinfeldt gone, the Cubs had lost three important cogs in their dynasty. For most of 1911, they were missing two more when Johnny Evers sat out most of the season because of a nervous breakdown and injuries limited manager Frank Chance to just 31 games. Clearly, storm clouds were gathering over baseball's most successful franchise in the first decade of the 20th century.

Chance was something of an afterthought at the start of his career in Chicago, and his career at first base happened by accident. Cubs manager Frank Selee wanted to use Johnny Kling as the team's regular catcher, and Chance was moved out from behind the plate to the outfield to make room. By 1903, Selee was searching for a solution at first base when rookie Bill Hanlon flopped. Chance was the answer, and he responded by batting .327 and leading the league with 67 stolen bases.

A year later, he batted .310, and when Selee fell ill and was forced to leave the team in 1905, the players elected Chance as his replacement. He batted .316 that year but led the league in an ominous category when he was hit by pitches 17 times. It was the beginning of a pattern that followed Chance throughout his career.

Chance managed the Cubs for seven and a half years, and his teams had a .664 winning percentage. But it was not smooth sailing. Despite his great success as manager, Chance had a bittersweet time in Chicago. In addition to the litany of injuries, including his repeated beanings, there were constant battles with ownership, most notably over his salary. After getting into a shouting match with owner Charles Murphy, Chance was either fired or resigned—there are differing accounts. By 1913, the man they called the "Peerless Leader" was managing the New York Yankees.

Chance was unhappy from the start in New York and left the Yankees in 1914, heading home to California where he ran an orange grove in Glendora, California. There was a brief stay as manager of the Los Angeles Angels after he purchased a one-third interest in the minor league team.

In 1923, Chance returned to the majors to manage the Boston Red Sox for one season. The next year, he was hired to manage the Chicago White Sox, a turn of events that did not exactly amuse the Cubs. But he developed bronchial asthma and died on September 15, 1924. He was just 47 years old.

Like Chance, Johnny Evers had an edge about him. But he was a student of the baseball rulebook, and his heads-up play at second base won plenty of games for the Cubs. Evers came to the Cubs in 1902 as a shortstop, but manager Frank Selee moved him to second base after just three days, pairing him with Joe Tinker to form a legendary double-play combination. He batted .293 and stole 25 bases in his first full season.

Evers's exit from Chicago had some interesting twists and turns. He suffered a nervous breakdown after losing $25,000 in a business venture, forcing the Cubs to use the often-unpredictable Heinie Zimmerman at second base in 1911. But Tinker to Zimmerman to Chance didn't quite have the same lyrical ring to it as Tinker to Evers to Chance. Evers recovered to enjoy his best season in 1912 when he batted .341, but his time in Chicago was nearing its end.

With Chance out, Evers got a five-year contract to manage the team. It was a bad idea. There were divisions in the clubhouse that sometimes deteriorated into fisticuffs with Evers right in the middle. The five-year deal to manage the team lasted for just one season, after which the second baseman either was fired or quit. There was an aborted trade to Boston when Evers refused to report. With the new Federal League beckoning, National League owners nullified the trade and allowed Evers to make his own deal with Boston. That enabled him to be part of the 1914 Miracle Braves, who came back from last place on July 4 to win the pennant. Evers was the centerpiece of the team, and after batting .438 in the World Series against Philadelphia, he won the Chalmers Award as league Most Valuable Player.

Joe Tinker came to the Cubs in 1902 and was the survivor among a dozen shortstops tried out by manager Frank Selee. In

1908, the Cubs' last world championship season, Tinker led his team in hits (146), triples (14), home runs (6), RBIs (68), and slugging percentage (.391). He continued to flourish at bat with 69 RBIs in both 1910 and 1911 and 75 in 1912.

Then owner Charles Murphy decided to make Johnny Evers the Cubs manager. Tinker was outraged at the idea that Evers, his longtime clubhouse rival, would be his boss. He demanded a trade and was sent to Cincinnati in an eight-player deal. Tinker became the team's player-manager in 1913, and although the Reds struggled through a 64–89 season, Tinker thrived, batting a career-best .317.

A year later, when Reds management decided to send a spy along with the club on road trips, Tinker refused to sign a new contract and jumped to the Federal League, the first prominent player to sign with the rival circuit. He became player-manager of the Chicago Whales, who finished second in 1914 and won the pennant the next year, outdrawing Tinker's old employers, the Cubs.

But the Federal League was in financial trouble and folded after 1915, leaving the Cubs free to stage a reunion with Tinker by making him manager. That lasted just one year, a fifth-place finish in 1916, before Tinker moved on, first to Columbus and then Orlando where he was part owner of minor league teams.

Meanwhile, Evers could not maintain his 1914 production in Boston. There were injuries and suspensions, and he seemed headed for another nervous breakdown. He soon drifted to Philadelphia and the Boston Red Sox, but by 1921, he was back in Chicago, managing first the Cubs and then the White Sox but without much success with either team.

In 1946, the old double-play trio, Tinker, Evers, and Chance, were elected to the Hall of Fame together. Chance had died in 1924, Evers died in 1947, and Tinker died in 1948 on his 68th birthday.

Even with Overall leading the exodus of Kling, Steinfeldt, Tinker, Evers, and Chance, the Cubs still had the best pitching staff in baseball, headed by Brown.

With a right hand missing his index finger and with two other fingers bent out of shape because of childhood accidents, Brown's pitches behaved differently, puzzling batters. He won 239 games and compiled a career earned run average of 2.06, lowest of any pitcher who threw 3,000 career innings.

Surrounded by a new cast, Brown was still a productive pitcher in 1911 despite a preseason knee injury, winning 21 games and saving 13 others for a Chicago team that finished in second place. But there were storm clouds with his earned run average at 2.80, nearly a run more than the Cubs were accustomed to from him. In 1912, Frank Chance's last year as manager, Brown's knee limited him to just eight starts. He was 5–6, distinctly ordinary numbers for the man who had been one of the National League's most dominant pitchers.

The Cubs sold Brown to Louisville of the American Association, but before the 1913 season, old pal Joe Tinker, now managing Cincinnati, purchased the pitcher. Brown went 11–12 with a 2.91 ERA for the last-place Reds It was a one-year cameo for Brown, and with the Federal League lusting for big names, he signed with the St. Louis Terriers as player-manager. The player part produced a 12–6 record and 3.29 ERA. The manager part did not work out as well, and with the Terriers in seventh place, Brown was replaced as manager by Fielder Jones, whose 1906 Hitless Wonder White Sox had spoiled the first year of the Last Chicago Cubs Dynasty.

Out at St. Louis, Brown drifted to the Brooklyn Tip Tops where he went 2–5. The next year, with Tinker surfacing as manager of the Federal League Chicago Whales, Brown signed on and showed his old-time form, going 17–8 with a 2.09 ERA and helping the Whales win the last Federal League pennant.

When the Feds folded, Tinker and Brown returned to the Cubs, a kind of heartwarming reunion that didn't exactly produce the hoped-for results. Tinker was the player-manager but appeared in just seven games, and his team finished in fifth place, a fat 26½ games behind. Brown went 2–3 in a season highlighted by one final showdown with longtime rival Christy Mathewson, who by then was managing the Cincinnati Reds.

Brown, now 40 and just a shadow of what he had once been, pitched for two more seasons with Columbus of the American Association and then became player-manager for Terre Haute of the Three-I League. When he went 16–6 with a 2.88 ERA, he moved to Indianapolis for the stretch run. Brown returned to Terre Haute in 1920, finishing his professional career in the same city where it started in 1901.

In retirement, Brown stayed in Terre Haute, eventually saving enough money to invest in the ball club that had given him his start. He died February 14, 1948, at the age of 71.

There is no question that Brown was the ace of the Cubs staff, but Ed Reulbach had a curve every bit as puzzling for hitters. Further complicating the task for batters was the right-hander's high leg kick and ability to hide the ball in his windup. Sometimes, the ball came up to the plate so quickly that hitters had no time to get set.

Reulbach was born in Detroit and played baseball and basketball at Notre Dame. He broke the school's single-season record for strikeouts in 1904. He was named captain of the team in 1905, but that summer, pitching in Vermont's Northern League, he fell in love and chose to leave Notre Dame to attend medical school at the University of Vermont. Four starts into his Vermont pitching career, the Cubs swept in and signed him.

He went 18–14 that season, winning nine straight games, pitching five shutouts with a 1.43 ERA. Then he became a vital cog in the Cubs run of three straight pennants from 1906 to 1908, leading the league in winning percentages all three years.

Reulbach struggled after that, although records of 12–8 in 1910, 16–9 in 1911, and 10–6 in 1912 might be considered perfectly respectable by modern baseball standards. They were not up to what the Cubs expected from him, and in July 1913, with his record 1–3, he was traded to Brooklyn. He had something of a renaissance with his new team, pitching effectively for an otherwise mediocre franchise.

Meanwhile, with the Superbas, Reulbach became something of a labor leader, organizing the Baseball Players Fraternity, a forerunner of today's Major League Players Association. Brooklyn management was not amused and released him in 1915. He signed with Newark of the Federal League and went 21–10 with a 2.23 ERA. Included was a 12-inning win over old pal "Three Finger" Brown and a 6–0 shutout over Baltimore in the final game of Federal League history. When the Federal League disbanded, Reulbach's rights were acquired by the Pittsburgh Pirates, who sold him to Boston where he pitched mostly in relief at the end of a brilliant career.

Reulbach ended his career with Providence of the International League in 1917. He spent a fortune trying to help his constantly ill son. The child died in 1931, leaving the pitcher deeply depressed by his loss. Reulbach died at age 78 on July 17, 1961.

"Three Finger" Brown was not alone as a dominant pitcher for the Cubs. Their whole rotation posed problems for National League hitters. When Chicago won 116 games in 1906, Brown led the staff with 26 victories. Right behind him, however, were Jack Pfiester, who went 20–8; Ed Reulbach, who was 19–4; Carl Lundgren, with 17 wins; and Orval Overall and Jack Taylor, who each won 12 games. The team's earned run average was a dazzling 1.76.

Lundgren came to Chicago from the University of Illinois where he was a civil engineering student, captain of the baseball team, and president of his senior class. Lundgren had can't-miss credentials, and the Cubs signed him right out of college. He won a spot in the rotation immediately and went 9–9 with a 1.97 ERA and 17 complete games in 18 starts as a rookie.

Lundgren was surrounded by 20-game winners Jack Taylor, Jake Weimer, and Bob Wicker at the start of his career. One by one, however, the Cubs disposed of those pitchers and replaced them with the Dynasty core of Brown, Reulbach, and Overall. With all the change around him, Lundgren was the holdover. He won 30 games over the next two seasons but had a tendency to wear down when the weather heated up. He finished with 91 wins over eight seasons with the Cubs.

In 1913, Lundgren was hired to coach baseball at the University of Michigan, succeeding Branch Rickey. At Michigan, he coached Hall of Famer George Sisler and won Big Ten Conference championships in each of his last three seasons. He left Michigan in 1920 to return to his alma mater, the University of Illinois, where he coached for 14 more years.

Jack Taylor may have been the most interesting case on the Cubs pitching staff. He had a reputation for finishing what he started, assembling an unbelievable streak of 187 consecutive complete games from 1901 to 1906. There was a 19-inning complete game and another that went 18 innings; there were complete games in both ends of a doubleheader; and he had a remarkable 278 complete games in 286 career starts. He pitched in a number of minor league cities until retiring in 1913. After baseball, Taylor worked as a coal miner. He died of cancer on March 4, 1938, at the age of 64.

Even though they won 116 games in 1906, the Cubs had just two 20-game winners that season: Brown and Jack Pfiester. At a time when the Cubs were in an annual tug-of-war at the top of the National League standings with the New York Giants, Pfiester had the reputation of handling their toughest rivals. That is, until the 1908 playoff game, when he was chased from the mound in the first inning and rescued by Brown, who pitched the Cubs to the pennant that day.

Pfiester pitched semipro ball around Cincinnati and then had two seasons of minor league ball, catching the attention of the Pittsburgh Pirates in 1903, when he struck out 195 batters in 288 innings with San Francisco of the Pacific Coast League. After two undistinguished cameo shots with the Pirates, he returned to the minors with Omaha of the Western League and blossomed, winning 49 games in two seasons and showing enough to interest the Cubs. In Chicago, he became the perfect left-handed complement to the right-handed Brown and produced 20 victories in 1906, his first season with the team, as the Cubs stomped through the National League to the pennant. It was his only 20-win season, but he compiled a 2.02 earned run average over eight seasons in Chicago, third best in history for pitchers with at least 1,000 innings. And most importantly, he went 15–5 with seven shutouts against the hated Giants.

Pfiester went just 12–10 in 1908 and recovered to go 17–6 in 1909, but he was never a dominant pitcher again. Illness and injuries limited him for the next two seasons, and the Cubs shuffled him off to Louisville. There was a brief recall to Chicago when the Cubs planned to sell him to Milwaukee. But a misdirected Western Union telegram caused the deal to fall through. Pfiester sued the telegraph company and collected a $2,000 settlement. After a cameo appearance with Sioux City of the Western League, the left-hander retired to Loveland, Ohio, where he died of a blood ailment at age 75 on September 3, 1953.

At the start of the Last Chicago Cubs Dynasty, the outfield was consistently Jimmy Slagle, Jimmy Sheckard, and Frank Schulte. They even occupied the first three spots in the batting order.

Slagle was called Rabbit, a tribute to his speed. He was the first to leave the Last Chicago Cubs Dynasty outfield, where he played from 1902 to 1908. He had stints with Washington, Philadelphia, and Boston before settling in with the Cubs. His speed made him the perfect leadoff man, and he knew how to use it, stealing 41 bases in his first season in Chicago and finishing his career with 274. He set a record in the 1907 World Series with six stolen bases that lasted until 1967 when it was broken by Lou Brock. He also had the first straight steal of home in World Series play.

Slagle's career in Chicago ended after the 1908 World Series. He was 35, and the Cubs had a capable replacement, Solly Hofman, ready to take over. Slagle returned to his roots, tiny Worthville, a map-dot town in western Pennsylvania, where he delighted in entertaining his friends and neighbors with tales of his life in the big leagues. A monument stands there to remember the town's only Major League player. He died in Chicago on May 10, 1956, at the age of 82.

Jimmy Sheckard was a marvelously talented outfielder, who seemed able to excel in all areas of the game. He was a skilled hitter and fielder who, at various times, led the National League in triples, home runs, slugging, runs, on-base percentage, walks, and stolen bases.

Sheckard broke in with Brooklyn in 1897 and stayed there until 1905 when he was traded to Chicago for four players and $2,000. It was just in time for him to join the start of the Last Chicago Cubs Dynasty. He led the league with 77 stolen bases in 1899 and again with 67 in 1903 when he also led the league with nine home runs.

In 1911, the year after the Cubs dynasty's last pennant, Sheckard led the league with 147 walks and 121 runs scored. The next year, his 122 walks led the league again, but when his batting average dipped to .245, he became trade bait and was sold to St.

Louis. From there, he moved on to Cincinnati, his last Major League stop.

After stops in Cleveland and Reading, Pennsylvania, as a minor league manager, Sheckard returned to Chicago as a Cubs coach. During World War I, he was athletic director at the Great Lakes Naval Training Station. Later he did some managing in semipro ball and coached the sport at Franklin and Marshall College. In January 1947, he was on his way to work, walking on a country road in Lancaster, Pennsylvania, when he was struck by a car. He died of his injuries at the age of 68.

Frank Schulte was the Cubs' resident slugger, leading the league in home runs twice and hitting 91 in 12 seasons with Chicago, big numbers during baseball's Deadball Era. He became a Cub almost by accident. Frank Selee, manager of the team, had dispatched scout George Huff to look at another outfield prospect in 1904, but Huff was more impressed with Schulte and brought him back to Chicago instead. In his debut, four days after his 22nd birthday, Schulte had five hits in a doubleheader at Philadelphia, establishing himself as a centerpiece in the Cubs lineup.

Schulte did his best to keep the Last Chicago Cubs Dynasty going after the team's appearance in the 1910 World Series. After leading the league with 10 home runs that season, he upped his production to 21 homers, including four grand slams, 107 runs batted in, and a .534 slugging percentage in 1911. He also became the first Major League player to have 20 doubles, 20 triples, 20 home runs, and 20 stolen bases in a single season. It was a unique accomplishment unmatched until 1957 when Willie Mays did it. The offensive outburst earned Schulte the Chalmers Trophy, the Deadball Era's equivalent of the Most Valuable Player. But with a diminished roster around Schulte, the Cubs dipped to second place, the beginning of a downward spiral that lasted 18 years.

The Cubs flourished with Schulte's productive bat in the middle of the lineup. In the team's four World Series appearances, he batted .309 and enjoyed a 13-game hitting streak. But his production began to dip after that magical 1911 season, and in 1916 the Cubs traded him to Pittsburgh, eliminating one more piece of their dynasty team. There were cameo appearances with Philadelphia and Washington followed by minor league stints in Baltimore, Syracuse, and Oakland, where he settled after his baseball career was done. He died there at age 67 on October 2, 1949.

Schulte's departure marked the official end of the Last Chicago Cubs Dynasty. He was the last man standing from the championship team's roster, and when he was traded it marked the end of the most successful team in the history of the franchise. The Cubs have been trying to replicate it ever since.

10

FACES OF THE FRANCHISE—OLD AND NEW

CAP ANSON (1879–1898)

To tell the truth, Adrian "Cap" Anson never wanted to play in Chicago. But once he got there, he stayed for 22 brilliant seasons as a Hall of Fame player and pennant-winning manager.

In college at Notre Dame, Anson organized the school's first baseball team and played third base well enough to earn a professional contract. He played a year at Rockford, Illinois, before moving to Philadelphia in 1872. When William Hulbert was organizing his new Chicago franchise, he imported pitcher Albert Spalding from Boston. It didn't take long for Anson to make himself right at home with his new team. By 1879, he had been appointed manager, or captain, leading to his nickname. Starting in 1880, he led the team to five pennants in seven years while at the same time batting over .300 every season as the team's first baseman. His 1880 team went 67–17, a .798 pace that has never been matched. Anson was a martinet as manager, with strict rules for his players, including a no-drinking edict that made him unpopular with the team. But there can be no denying that under

Anson, Chicago's National League team became baseball's first dynasty.

Anson was an innovator on the field, introducing spring training, the hit-and-run play, signals, platoons, and a pitching rotation. Meanwhile, as a player, Anson was in a class by himself. He batted over .300 24 times in a 27-year career and was credited with becoming the first player in history to accumulate 3,000 hits. That achievement was later questioned by researchers who claimed he benefited from some overly friendly scoring and credit him instead with 2,995 hits. If he had known that was going to happen, he probably would have stuck around to get the extra five hits.

A deadly two-strike hitter, he led the league in hitting four times and in runs batted in eight times. He hit three consecutive homers in one game and five in two games. He hit four doubles in a game and scored six runs in another. He had five or more hits in a game 10 times. When he retired, he held records in a fistful of categories including hits, at-bats, doubles, and runs.

Flushed with his success, Chicago gave Anson a 10-year contract in 1888. But he never won another pennant and came under increasing scrutiny from the team's new owner, Jim Hart. For his part, Anson criticized his players, blaming them for the team's failures and calling them "a bunch of drunkards and loafers."[1] So, despite managing Chicago for more than 1,200 wins and five championships, his stay in the city ended as it had begun, with some bad feelings on both sides.

ERNIE BANKS (1953–1971)

It is probably fair to say that Ernie Banks never had a bad day at the ballpark. He would arrive for games with a perpetual smile on his face, delighted that he would have another chance to play a kids game. That was his job—to play a little boys game. And from start to finish, he played it with a boundless joy and verve rarely seen on Major League ball fields.

It didn't matter that in his 19-year career, Banks never played in a World Series and only occasionally played on a team that contended. He still excelled, hitting 512 home runs and winning consecutive Most Valuable Player awards in 1958 and 1959 while playing on also-ran teams.

Banks would arrive in the Cubs clubhouse, look around at teammates struggling through a tough season, and announce in a joyful voice for all to hear, "It's a great day for a ballgame, so let's play two."[2] He became known as "Mr. Cub," and a statue of him stands outside of Wrigley Field. It is a tribute to a player who arrived out of the Negro Leagues in 1953 and hit the first batting practice pitch he saw into the left-field bleachers at Wrigley.

After a 10-game cameo in 1953, the Cubs installed Banks at shortstop the next season, and he responded with 19 home runs. It began a 19-year love affair with the fans of Chicago. In six of his first seven years with the Cubs, Banks led the league in games played. There were 44 home runs in his second full season, part of a stretch of more than 40 home runs in five of the next six years. He led the league with 47 in 1958 and 41 in 1960.

Banks was an anomaly, a shortstop with long ball potential. He had a spindly build that belied his power. Blessed with quick wrists, he snapped at pitches, and many of his home runs were line drives instead of high, arching fly balls. He quickly became one of the most dangerous hitters in the National League, driving in over 100 runs eight times.

His first Most Valuable Player award in 1958 was constructed on a season in which he batted .313 and led the National League with 47 home runs and 129 runs batted in. The next year, he hit 45 homers and drove in 143 and became the fifth player to win consecutive MVP awards. He holds Cubs career records for extra base hits (1,009) and holds the record for the most home runs (277) by a National League shortstop.

Halfway through his career, the Cubs decided he had lost some range at shortstop and shifted him to first base. It made little difference to Mr. Cub. He was still playing baseball, still smiling, and hoping they'd let him play two.

PHIL CAVARRETTA (1934–1955)

When Phil Cavarretta arrived in Chicago as a 19-year-old rookie in 1935, it didn't take long for player-manager Charlie Grimm to surrender his job at first base and move into the dugout. Cavarretta was that good.

Coming out of high school in Chicago, he signed with Peoria, Illinois, of the Central League and hit for the cycle in his first professional game. Two months after he turned 18, he was in the big leagues and had eight hits in 23 at-bats in a cameo appearance in 1934. A year later, he was the regular first baseman on a pennant-winning team that ran off 21 straight victories in September to nail down the flag. It was a quick turnaround for a kid who used to stand outside Wrigley Field, waiting for players to sign autographs.

Cavarretta struggled in the 1935 World Series against Detroit, managing just three hits in 24 at-bats, but thrived in two other postseason appearances, batting .462 against the New York Yankees in 1938 and .423 against Detroit in 1945. It was in 1945 that Cavarretta had a personal Triple Crown, leading the National League in hitting with a .355 batting average, winning the Most Valuable Player award, and playing in the World Series.

He was a hometown hero, beloved by the fans and a fixture with the Cubs for two decades during which he compiled a .293 batting average. His status led to him being named player-manager of the team in 1951, succeeding Frank Frisch. The problem was that he inherited a bad Cubs team that was in the midst of a decade in which they never finished higher than fifth in the eight-team league. After being publicly pessimistic about the team's prospects for 1954, Cavarretta became the first modern manager to be fired during spring training. He finished his career across town, playing two years with the White Sox.

FRANK CHANCE (1898–1914)

Frank Chance played first base with a chip on his shoulder and managed the Cubs the same way. Still, he compiled formidable statistics in both jobs during the Last Chicago Cubs Dynasty.

His success earned him the nickname the "Peerless Leader," and his four pennants in five years, including a record 116 victories in 1906, marked the best five-year stretch for any team in baseball history. In Chance's seven and a half seasons as manager, the Cubs compiled a .664 winning percentage, a franchise record. Still, he was cranky from the start when his manager, Frank Selee, decided to move him from catcher-outfielder to first base. Chance threatened to retire. He had other options—he had studied to be a dentist and was an outstanding amateur boxer, admired by the professional fighters of the time. But baseball was his choice, and a sweetened contract convinced him to stay as the Cubs constructed the legendary double-play combination of Tinker to Evers to Chance.

When Selee fell ill in 1905, the players voted to have Chance succeed him as manager. A year later, when the team went on its tear through the National League, he took matters into his own hands during a game against the Cincinnati Reds. Standing on first base, he took off and stole second. On the next pitch, he took off again, stealing third and then home. It was called baseball's most expensive steal when owner Charles Murphy decided to reward Chance with 10 percent ownership of the club. Chance, however, claimed he had to pay for the stake in the team and complained about being underpaid compared to other managers like John McGraw of the Giants and Fred Clarke of the Pirates. He later sold the 10 percent for $150,000.

In the field, Chance was a productive player, compiling a career batting average of .296 with 401 stolen bases. He stole 67 bases in 1903 and 57 in 1906 when he led the league with 103 runs scored.

Chance liked to crowd the plate and was frequently hit by pitches, including five times in a doubleheader against Cincinnati. He was hit by pitches 137 times in 17 seasons. All the beanings added up, and he lost the hearing in one ear. He was diagnosed with blood clots on his brain and underwent surgery. While hospitalized, he got into a shouting match with Murphy over the owner's penurious payroll policies. Chance moved on to briefly manage the New York Yankees and Boston Red Sox but never again experienced the success he had in Chicago.

JOHNNY EVERS (1902–1917, 1922, 1929)

The middle man on the Tinker to Evers to Chance double-play unit during the Last Chicago Cubs Dynasty was Johnny Evers, known in baseball circles as the Crab because, well, he was not the most pleasant fellow to be around. Evers played with an edge, a bad attitude that often had him at odds with umpires, opponents, and even his own teammates.

A career .270 hitter, Evers was at his best in the World Series, batting .350 in both the 1907 and 1908 Series. He was also fast on the bases, stealing 324 bases in 18 seasons, including four in one game on June 16, 1907. He played just 46 games in 1911 but bounced back to bat .341 in 1912, fourth best in the National League, and was named manager of the team the next season.

The Cubs finished third, but Evers was fired anyway and dealt to Boston just in time to be an integral part of the Miracle Braves, who recovered from being in last place on July 4 to win the pennant and sweep the World Series against Philadelphia. Evers was voted the National League's Most Valuable Player and had another banner World Series, batting .438.

Injuries and suspensions limited Evers's contribution after that. By 1921, he was back with the Cubs, named manager for a second time. Like his stint in 1913, it lasted just one year. When the team finished seventh, the Crab was dismissed.

STAN HACK (1932–1947)

For the better part of 16 years in the 1930s and 1940s, Stan Hack provided an anchor at third base for the Cubs. He was a consistent .300 hitter, topping that mark six times and compiling a career batting average of .301. He was also the centerpiece of one of the more disappointing episodes in the team's World Series history.

In the 1935 World Series, Detroit was up three games to two, and the Cubs needed a win in Game Six to stay alive. With the game tied at 3–3, Hack, who batted .348 in three World Series, opened the ninth inning with a triple. Now the Cubs were perfectly positioned to get the go-ahead run home and perhaps force a Game Seven, but it never happened. Billy Jurges struck out. Then manager Charlie Grimm decided to let pitcher Larry French bat for himself, and he bounced out with Hack still holding at third. When Augie Galan flied out, the threat was over and Detroit scored a run in the bottom of the ninth to win the game and the World Series.

Normally a leadoff man, Hack twice led the league in hits, twice led in stolen bases, and had a stretch of six years from 1936 to 1941 when he scored over 100 runs. He was a left-handed batter and a patient hitter. He had nearly 1,100 walks but just 466 strikeouts in 7,278 at-bats.

Hack was one of the Cubs' most popular players, quick with a smile. But he walked away from the team in 1943 after repeated squabbles with manager Jimmie Wilson. When Grimm replaced Wilson in 1944, Hack returned and led the team to its last World Series the next year when he hit .323 and scored 110 runs. Once again, Chicago played Detroit in the Series and Hack batted .367, but the Tigers won in seven games.

Appointed manager of the Cubs during spring training in 1954, his teams struggled, finishing seventh, seventh, and eighth in his three years. The problem may have been they never had a third baseman as good as Stan Hack was during his playing days.

GABBY HARTNETT (1922–1941)

In baseball's early days, catchers had a reputation. Their main duty was defense, handling pitchers and throwing out base runners. Leave the hitting to the other seven guys in the lineup. Gabby Hartnett was part of a generation of catchers who changed all that.

Hartnett could hit. So could contemporaries like Mickey Cochrane and Bill Dickey. It was Hartnett, however, who became the first catcher to reach 200 home runs and 1,000 runs batted in. And he was the only one of the three to hold a blatant conversation with renowned Chicago gangster Al Capone, an episode that greatly displeased Commissioner Kenesaw Mountain Landis.

After just one season in the minors, Hartnett was purchased by the Cubs in 1922. Two years later, when Bob O'Farrell suffered a fractured skull, Hartnett became the first string catcher and quickly established himself as one of the most dangerous hitters in the National League, hitting .299 with 16 home runs in 111 games. He hit 24 homers the next year, batted over .300 six times, and finished with a .297 career batting average and 236 career home runs.

Hartnett's best season was 1930, a year in which hitters dominated baseball. He batted .339 with career highs of 37 home runs and 122 runs batted in. Five years later, he helped the Cubs to the pennant when he batted .344 and won the National League Most Valuable Player award. He batted a career-best .354 in 1937 that included a 26-game hitting streak.

Blessed with a strong throwing arm, Hartnett was not shy about showing it off. He sometimes teased runners, shouting "Go ahead! Run!" and then delighted in throwing them out. In 20 seasons, he threw out 56 percent of runners who attempted to steal and five times threw out 60 percent or more of attempted base stealers.

Hartnett was also behind the plate for several memorable moments in baseball history. He was the catcher when Babe Ruth either did or did not call his home run in the 1932 World Series. Hartnett always insisted that Ruth was merely indicating that he had one strike left in the at-bat. He was also the National League catcher for the first All-Star Game in 1933 and was behind the plate for Carl Hubbell's five straight strikeouts of Hall of Famers Ruth, Lou Gehrig, Jimmie Foxx, Al Simmons, and Joe Cronin in the 1934 All-Star Game.

Hartnett is known for his game-winning "homer in the gloamin'" in 1938 that propelled the Cubs into first place. Within a week, they had won the pennant and were in the World Series.

Hartnett managed Chicago for just two more seasons. By 1941, he was released and spent his final Major League season with the New York Giants, hitting .300 in 64 games. He retired with a .489 slugging average, at the time highest in history for a catcher.

FERGUSON JENKINS (1965–1983)

There's an old adage in baseball that the most important pitch of an at-bat is strike one. Ferguson Jenkins was pretty good at strike two and strike three as well. Jenkins struck out more than 3,000 batters (3,192) and did it while walking less than 1,000 (997), a brilliant ratio matched by just four other pitchers in history— Greg Maddux, Pedro Martinez, Curt Schilling, and John Smoltz.

Jenkins's best season was 1971 when he won 24 games and was the National League's Cy Young Award winner. He struck out 263 batters that season and walked just 37. He led the league with 325 innings pitched and 30 complete games, one of four times he led the league in that category. He had a history of finishing what he started with 267 complete games to his credit. And in the pre–designated hitter era, he could hit, too. Jenkins hit six home runs that season, including two in one game, and drove in 20 runs. He finished with 13 career homers.

Without benefit of a World Series, Jenkins's best baseball main event performance came in the 1967 All-Star Game when he pitched three innings and struck out six American League slug-gers—Mickey Mantle, Jim Fregosi, Tony Oliva, Harmon Kille-brew, Tony Conigliaro, and Rod Carew.

Jenkins was also a bit of a hard-luck pitcher, losing 13 games by a score of 1–0 and losing 45 games when his team was shut out.

Jenkins grew up in Canada playing basketball and hockey and running track as well as playing baseball. He lived across the street from a coal yard and often spent spare time hurling pieces of coal and rocks at an ice chute, an activity that improved his accuracy.

He signed with the Philadelphia Phillies in 1962, working mostly out of the bullpen when he reached the majors. When he came to the Cubs, they converted him to a starter, and beginning in 1967, he had a streak of six straight 20-win seasons, equaling a

Cubs record set six decades before by Mordecai "Three Finger" Brown.

Traded to Texas in 1974, he responded with a 25-win season and 29 complete games, both leading the league. He also logged time in Boston before returning to the Cubs to complete his career. He finished with 284 wins and a 3.34 earned run average.

RYNE SANDBERG (1981–1994, 1996–1997)

Ballplayers will tell you that there are days when they are in a zone at the plate, when pitches come in looking as big as balloons, begging to be hit. For Ryne Sandberg, June 23, 1984, was one of those days.

Sandberg was in his third Major League season and had accumulated some solid credentials, including the first of nine straight Gold Gloves at second base and two straight years with over 30 stolen bases. But he had yet to show much more than average ability at the plate. That would all change on that June afternoon with a national television audience watching.

The Cubs were playing the St. Louis Cardinals on NBC's *Game of the Week*. Chicago was trailing 9–8 in the ninth inning when Sandberg tied the score with a home run against Hall of Fame closer Bruce Sutter. The Cardinals scored two runs in the 10th inning, and Sandberg responded in the bottom of the 10th with a two-run homer to tie the score again in a game Chicago would win 12–11 in 11 innings. Sandberg finished the day with five hits in six at-bats, seven runs batted in, and two runs scored. He was no longer just average. Manager Jim Frey saw Sandberg's long ball potential even before that and encouraged the young second baseman to relax and swing hard.

Sandberg went on to win the Most Valuable Player trophy that season, batting .314 with 200 hits, 114 runs, 36 doubles, 19 triples, 19 home runs, and 84 runs batted in. He also stole 32 bases.

After that breakout season, Sandberg was viewed as the best second baseman of his generation with 10 straight All-Star selections. His career did not start out that way.

Drafted in the 20th round by Philadelphia in 1978, he demonstrated a sure glove in three minor league seasons before coming up to the Phillies in 1981. He played 13 games that September and was projected as a third baseman. But the Phillies already had Hall of Famer Mike Schmidt firmly entrenched at that position. Meanwhile, Dallas Green, who had drafted Sandberg, had left the Philadelphia organization to run the Cubs, and one of his first moves was to trade for the infielder. Sandberg's stay with the Cubs did not exactly get off to a rousing start when he managed just one hit in his first 32 at-bats. He recovered to bat .271 and led the team with 32 stolen bases and 103 runs scored. And things got better after that.

His breakout season in 1984 was followed by a consistent display of long ball punch. He had nine straight years with double digits in home runs, including a league-leading 40 in 1990 and 25 in 1996 after he left the game for a year. He sat out the 1995 season, saying he felt he could no longer play up to the standards he had set at the position. But he came back in 1996 for two more seasons with the Cubs, ending his career with a .285 batting average, 282 home runs, 344 stolen bases, and a ticket to the Hall of Fame. He would later return to the Major Leagues as manager of the Philadelphia Phillies, the team that dealt him away in 1982.

RON SANTO (1960–1974)

Playing with a secret, Ron Santo was one of baseball's best third basemen in a 15-year career, 14 of them with the Cubs. Before he ever got to the Major Leagues, Santo was diagnosed with diabetes, a disease that eventually took his life.

Santo never let on that he had the ailment, careful to hide it from teammates as he wove a Hall of Fame career that included five Gold Gloves and a Major League record for leading the league in total chances nine times. He also led the league in assists seven times and in double plays six times and was a nine-time All-Star selection. And despite his medical condition, he missed just 23 of a possible 1,595 games in the decade of the 1960s.

And he could hit. He batted .300 with 30 home runs four times and had a lifetime batting average of .277 with 342 home runs and 1,331 runs batted in. He was just the second third baseman to reach 300 home runs, joining Hall of Famer Eddie Mathews, and his numbers earned him election to the Hall of Fame. Included in his home run totals were five grand slams. One of the unlikeliest came when Santo felt a diabetic reaction coming on as he waited his at-bat in the on-deck circle. Billy Williams kept fouling balls off, and Santo, unable to get back to the dugout for a candy bar to quell the sugar problem, slowly felt his strength waning. Finally, he came to bat with the bases loaded, and barely able to muster enough strength to swing the bat, Santo connected for a grand-slam home run.

Santo was one of Chicago's most popular players. During the 1969 season, he would often celebrate Cubs victories by jumping in the air joyously and clicking his heels. The routine angered opponents but made the third baseman a Chicago icon.

The Cubs signed Santo out of high school in Seattle in 1959, and a year later, he was in the Major Leagues. In his only minor league season at San Antonio, he led the Texas League with 153 putouts but also committed 53 errors. The Cubs preferred to concentrate on his .327 batting average, and halfway through 1960, he was in Chicago.

When the Cubs tried to trade Santo to California in 1973, he vetoed the deal, becoming the first player to invoke those newly won rights under the collective bargaining agreement. He wanted to stay in Chicago, and the Cubs obliged him with a trade to the White Sox. He stayed for just one season, retiring at the end of the 1974 season.

After his playing career, Santo was involved in a number of businesses before returning to the Cubs to work as a broadcaster in 1990. He served as a member of the Juvenile Diabetes Foundation's board of directors before his death following a heart attack in 2010.

ALBERT SPALDING (1876–1878)

Baseball's Renaissance man was Albert Spalding, who impacted the game as its first great pitcher and was then a manager, team president, and a sporting goods company founder.

In 1876, when William Hulbert launched his construction of the National League with its cornerstone franchise in Chicago, he recruited Albert Spalding, who was working for the Boston franchise at the time and dominating the old National Association. The Chicago team dominated the National League's first season with Spalding managing and won 47 games as the White Stockings (still some years away from changing their name to the Cubs) won the league's first championship.

The pitching workload took its toll on Spalding, and two years after arriving in Chicago, he retired as a player to concentrate on other endeavors, including his sporting goods company, which became the sole provider of equipment for the new league.

Spalding also exercised his options, first to manage the team and then to become the franchise president from 1882 through 1891. He led the battle against the upstart Players League, which folded after one season, and fought off a move to turn baseball into a monopoly through interlocking ownership. He also helped organize Chicago's World's Fair in 1893 and launched a commission to investigate the origins of baseball. Spalding was inducted into the Hall of Fame in 1939.

JOE TINKER (1902–1916)

When Frank Selee set about the business of constructing the Last Chicago Cubs Dynasty, the first piece of the puzzle was running a set of auditions for shortstop. Eventually, he settled on Joe Tinker, who wasn't exactly thrilled at winning the competition. That's because Tinker had played second base for Denver in 1900 and third base for Portland in 1901.

Born in Kansas in 1880, Tinker was an apprentice paperhanger and had bounced around the Midwest, playing for a succession of semipro teams. He began to attract serious Major League interest in 1901 when he batted .290 for Portland of the Western League. Chicago and Cincinnati inquired about the young third baseman, and Tinker preferred the Cubs.

The price of his position shift from third base to shortstop was high. Tinker committed 72 errors in his first season and 141 in his first two years on the job. But Tinker mastered it. The double-play combination of Tinker to Evers to Chance played together for the first time on September 13, 1902, and turned their first double play two days later.

By 1906, the year the Cubs won a record 116 games, Tinker led all National League shortstops with a .944 fielding percentage, the first of five times when he led the league in that category. He also led the league twice in assists and twice in putouts. On offense, he was fast and stole 336 bases in his career. He also was known for his ability to handle the bat: he was adept at a new baseball wrinkle called the hit-and-run, with the ability to push the ball through a position vacated by an infielder who had moved to cover a base.

Tinker had an uncanny ability to hit Christy Mathewson, perhaps the best pitcher of the generation. In the 1908 Fred Merkle game that ended in a controversial tie, Tinker accounted for the lone Chicago run with a home run against Mathewson, who won 37 games that season. When the teams had a pennant playoff game, Tinker's triple against Mathewson keyed a four-run rally. For his career, Tinker's batting average was .262. Against Mathewson, it was .350.

When the Cubs dismissed Frank Chance as their manager and replaced him with Evers, Tinker demanded to be traded. He was dealt to Cincinnati in an eight-player swap and took over the Reds as player-manager. The player part was fine. He batted a career high .317 with a .445 slugging percentage and .968 fielding percentage. The manager part was less successful as the Reds finished in seventh place at 64–89, and Tinker left for the new Federal League as player-manager of the Chicago Whales.

Tinker took the Whales to the pennant in 1915, but the league drowned in a sea of red ink, and by 1916, he was back with the Cubs as manager for one last season. He was inducted into the Hall of Fame in 1946 along with his old double-play pals, Johnny Evers and Frank Chance.

BILLY WILLIAMS (1959–1976)

Quietly, Billy Williams assembled a Hall of Fame career, playing in the shadow of more high-profile players. He grew up in Mobile, Alabama, preceded there by home run king Hank Aaron. When he got to Chicago, Ernie Banks owned the spotlight, and when he moved to Oakland, people spent most of their time talking about Reggie Jackson. Williams was an under-the-radar performer, always there, it seemed, supplying a big hit or a clutch play in the outfield. He was never flamboyant, but he was consistent.

A six-time All-Star, Williams finished his career with a .290 batting average, 426 home runs, and 1,475 runs batted in. He led the National League in hitting with a .333 average in 1972. He played in 1,117 consecutive games over seven seasons from 1963 to 1970, and manager Leo Durocher kept promising to find him a day off. "But every time I made out my lineup card, I had to put him in there," Durocher said. "It would be like scratching Whirlaway and Seabiscuit from a big race."[3]

Coming out of high school, Williams was a standout football player and was offered a scholarship to play defensive end at Grambling. He chose baseball instead, playing semipro ball in Mobile and attracting attention from the Cubs. After playing in San Antonio, he had cameo appearances in Chicago in 1959 and 1960, and he started in left field for the Cubs on June 15, 1961, his 23rd birthday. He hit a grand-slam homer to beat San Francisco and became an everyday performer after that.

Williams was Rookie of the Year that season, batting .278 with 25 home runs and 86 runs batted in, the first of 13 straight seasons in which he hit more than 20 homers and drove in at least 84 runs. He hit for the cycle in a 1968 game and had a streak of five straight home runs over two games that same year. When the Cubs blew a big lead and were overtaken by the New York Mets for the pennant in 1969, Williams hit .304 in September, the only Cub over .300 that month.

In 1970, Williams led the league with 205 hits and batted .322 with 42 home runs and 122 runs batted in and finished second to Johnny Bench in the Most Valuable Player balloting. Two years later, he won the batting title, hit 37 homers, drove in 122 runs, and again finished second to Bench in the MVP voting.

Traded to Oakland, Williams spent the last two years of his career with the As, hitting 34 home runs and driving in 122 runs, and was elected to the Hall of Fame in 1987.

HACK WILSON (1923–1934)

Built short and squat, Hack Wilson was the National League's version of Babe Ruth. And in 1930, he had a Ruthian season, batting .356, hitting 56 home runs, and driving in a record 191 runs.

Wilson was a compact five foot six and 190 pounds with size five and half feet that looked more suited to a ballerina than a ballplayer. He was barrel-chested and blessed with home run power. He led the league in homers four times in a 12-year career. Six of those years were spent with the Cubs after a clerical error by the New York Giants exposed him to the player draft in 1925. He had been optioned to Toledo by Giants manager John McGraw, who was tired of Wilson's affection for nightlife. The slugger enjoyed after-hour pursuits just as much in Chicago.

He was a consistent long-ball threat with 21 homers in his first season with the Cubs when he batted .321 and drove in 109 runs. The next year, he hit 30 homers and drove in 129. In 1929, he batted .345, hit 39 homers, and drove in 159, helping the Cubs to the National League pennant. Wilson produced one of baseball's most prodigious string of statistics in 1930, setting a National League home run record that lasted until the end of the 20th century and creating an RBI record that still stands 85 years later.

Through his years with the Cubs, Wilson had a safety net in manager Joe McCarthy, who often covered up for the slugger's affection for alcohol. But when McCarthy was replaced by a harsher Rogers Hornsby in 1931, Wilson was on his own. His production slipped dramatically, and he was traded away, first to St. Louis and then to Brooklyn, where he enjoyed a brief revival, batting .297 with 23 home runs and 123 RBIs. He even filled in at second base for five games, including an 18-inning marathon. He didn't make any errors there either. But he was clearly on the decline, and by 1935, just five years after he tore up the league,

Wilson was back in the minors, no longer the slugger he had once been. That was the same year that Babe Ruth's career ended as well.

11

THE OTHER GUYS

The Last Chicago Cubs Dynasty was not without its complications. Most of those were supplied by the Pittsburgh Pirates and New York Giants, each equipped with great players who, like the core of the Cubs, were headed to the Hall of Fame.

Before the Cubs won three straight pennants and four in five years, John McGraw's Giants were the best team in the National League with consecutive pennants in 1904 and 1905. McGraw was the most powerful man in baseball at the time, so powerful in fact that in a fit of pique, he nearly torpedoed the World Series by refusing to play the American League champions in 1904.

The Cubs might have captured five straight pennants—they won 104 games in 1909 but finished in second place—if it hadn't been for the Pirates, who interrupted their run by winning 110 that year. The Pirates won three straight pennants from 1901 to 1903, part of a stretch of 14 straight first division finishes under manager Fred Clarke, and played in the first World Series, a culmination to the baseball season that seemed like a great idea until McGraw briefly shot it down.

Pittsburgh and New York were blessed with great rosters. McGraw's Giants had Roger Bresnahan, a superior catcher; second baseman Larry Doyle; and a pitching staff that included Iron

Man Joe McGinnity, Hooks Wiltse, and the great Christy Mathewson. Clarke's Pirates countered with stars like third baseman Tommy Leach; pitchers Deacon Phillippe, Sam Leever, and Babe Adams; and perhaps the greatest shortstop in baseball history, Honus Wagner.

This, then, is the story of some of the other guys, the great players and teams that stood in the way of the Last Chicago Cubs Dynasty.

NEW YORK GIANTS

John McGraw

John McGraw was a handful, a bit of a grouch who played baseball with a nasty attitude and managed it the same way. He used tactics that were borderline at best and downright dirty at worst.

McGraw managed the Giants from 1902 to 1932, winning 10 pennants and three World Series. His teams finished first or second 21 times in his 29 full seasons, and his 2,763 victories as a manager are second only to Connie Mack's 3,731.

He was good at infuriating people. A favorite target was Pittsburgh owner Barney Dreyfuss. McGraw once offered to bet Dreyfuss $10,000, no small piece of change, on the outcome of a Giants-Pirates game and then abruptly withdrew the offer, saying everyone knew Dreyfuss did not always pay off gambling debts. The affair sent Dreyfuss into a frenzy, and he convinced National League president Harry Pulliam to suspend and fine McGraw. It was all worth it to the Giants manager because he had succeeded in getting under Dreyfuss's skin.

McGraw liked to shake things up, occasionally resulting in fines and suspensions. He was ejected from games 131 times, a record that stood into the 21st century when it was broken by Atlanta manager Bobby Cox. McGraw once threw a cup of water at umpire Bill Klem. Another time, he punched umpire Bill By-ron. Cox, Billy Martin, Earl Weaver, Leo Durocher, and other umpire baiters had nothing on him.

After bouncing around baseball for a while, McGraw surfaced in Baltimore, and it was there that he became a national figure. When the Orioles moved to the National League, he was their third baseman and leadoff hitter, batting over .320 for nine straight years and stealing 436 bases. He was fond of blocking the paths of base runners and occasionally tripping them, sometimes grabbing their belts to slow them down.

By age 26, McGraw was managing the Orioles and defied the baseball establishment, first by refusing a trade to Brooklyn and then by agreeing to play for the St. Louis Cardinals only if his contract language was stripped of the reserve clause. He was far ahead of his time in that fight, achieving in baseball's dark ages something other players did not accomplish until some seven decades later. After a year in St. Louis, he returned to Baltimore as manager and part owner of the team in Ban Johnson's new American League. He was constantly at odds with Johnson, and when the league boss suspended him in July 1902, McGraw sim-ply left the Orioles, jumping back to the National League to take over the Giants. He immediately dumped nine New York players and imported a fistful of Baltimore players, including Roger Bres-nahan and Joe McGinnity, who would prove vital to the Giants' success.

McGraw held grudges and displayed one of them in 1904. After Pittsburgh and Boston played in the first World Series in 1903, McGraw's Giants won the NL pennant in 1904. There would be no World Series, however, because McGraw would not participate against Boston, a team from old rival Ban Johnson's American League. The snub that almost destroyed the World Series in its infancy was typical of McGraw's cantankerous de-meanor. He was not a popular character, but few could top his baseball savvy. He is credited with helping develop the hit-and-run, the squeeze play, and other strategic innovations. He was also a master at infuriating opponents. He was an expert bench jockey and encouraged a swagger in his players that made them rather unpopular. He was, however, the most successful manager of baseball's Deadball Era.

Christy Mathewson

Christy Mathewson was Captain America and Frank Merriwell, a baseball hero when they were in short supply. At a time when the game was populated by what many considered to be the underbelly of society, transients, and ne'er-do-wells, Mathewson was a breath of fresh air, a college-educated, handsome man who said and did all the right things.

And he was also probably the best pitcher of baseball's Deadball Era.

Mathewson won 373 games in a 17-year career, compiling a 2.13 earned run average. There were a remarkable 37 wins in 1908—his fourth 30-win season—and 12 consecutive 20-win seasons. He led the league in earned run average five times, including a stunning 1.14 in 1909, and led the league in strikeouts five times. In the 1905 World Series, he threw three shutouts over six days to propel the Giants to the championship over Connie Mack's Philadelphia Athletics. Using a pitch he called the fade-away, which resembled today's screwball, Mathewson dominated baseball. The pitch behaved like a reverse curveball that darted away from hitters. Mixed with his fastball and traditional curveball, Mathewson baffled batters. His pinpoint control often made him almost unhittable.

In the three World Series shutouts against the Athletics, Mathewson allowed just 14 hits, walked one, and struck out 18. It was a virtuoso performance that left Mack in awe. Asked about the Giants ace years later, the A's manager said, "Mathewson was the greatest pitcher who ever lived. He had knowledge, judgment, perfect control and form. It was wonderful to watch him pitch when he wasn't pitching against you."[1]

His reputation preceded him before he reached New York. Mathewson was a star pitcher at Bucknell University where he also played center on the basketball team and fullback on the football team. He was president of his class, sang in the glee club, and played in the band.

Mathewson arrived in New York in 1900, one month before his 20th birthday. He lost his first two starts and lugged a 5.08 ERA off to Norfolk. That winter Cincinnati drafted him for $100 and then traded him back to the Giants in exchange for a washed-up Amos Rusie. Mathewson responded with a no-hitter against St. Louis in his first full season, when he won 20 games and became a mainstay on New York's pitching staff. His credo was simple. "You can learn little from victory," he once told sportswriter Grantland Rice. "You can learn everything from defeat."[2]

Manager John McGraw embraced Mathewson, often calling the pitcher the son he never had. When Mathewson began to break down at age 36, the pitcher made a request. He wanted to become a manager, and McGraw accommodated him with a trade to Cincinnati for Buck Herzog, a deal made on the condition that Mathewson replace Herzog as manager of the Reds. In 1916, Mathewson returned to the mound for one last outing to face his old nemesis "Three Finger" Brown. By then, Brown was 40; and Matty, 36, both shells of their former greatness. Mathewson allowed 15 hits but won the game 10–8 for his 373rd victory and the only one with any team other than the Giants.

Commissioned as a captain in World War I, Mathewson was exposed to mustard gas and developed tuberculosis. He died of the disease in 1925, on the first day of the World Series.

Joe McGinnity

They called Joe McGinnity Iron Man, but not because of his propensity for an inordinately heavy workload. Instead, it was because he spent the off-season working in an iron foundry. Still, the nickname certainly fit his baseball career when he might have been the hardest-working pitcher in the game.

McGinnity pitched 434 innings in 1903, more than double the typical workload of modern pitchers, and then followed that with 408 innings the next year. There were three straight seasons of 343 innings or more, and he completed 314 of 381 starts over a 10-year career. His crowning achievement, however, may have come in August 1903, when he started both ends of doubleheaders three times and won all six games. He pitched a pair of six-hitters, beating Boston 4–1 and 5–2 on August 1. Then he beat Brooklyn 6–1 and 4–3 on August 8 and punctuated the first game victory by stealing home for the game's first run. He completed the doubleheader trifecta by beating Philadelphia 4–1 and 9–2 on August 31.

In his Major League career, McGinnity had seven 20-win seasons and two 30-win seasons, and including his minor league career, he won more than 500 games. Now that's an Iron Man.

As a youngster, McGinnity worked in the coal mines of Illinois and Montana while also playing semipro baseball. By 1893, he had hooked on with Montgomery of the Southern League, and a year later, he was with Kansas City of the Western League. He was a mediocre pitcher and drifted back into semipro ball while working the mines and operating a saloon in Springfield, Illinois. It was during this time that McGinnity developed a unique pitch, a sort of sidearm curve ball he called "Old Sal." It was that pitch the led him back to professional baseball and eventually to the Major Leagues with the Baltimore Orioles, managed by John McGraw. In 1899, his rookie year, he went 28–16 to lead the

National League in wins and pitched 366⅓ innings. There was one week in October when he won five games in six days.

A year later, a number of Orioles, including McGinnity, migrated to Brooklyn to play for the Superbas. Again, the Iron Man flourished, leading the league with 29 wins, including 10 in a row, and throwing 343 innings. Next, McGinnity returned to Baltimore of the new American League to pitch for his old pal, McGraw. He was, however, developing a bit of an edge and a reputation for baiting umpires. In one episode, McGinnity spat at umpire Tim Connolly, resulting in a 12-day suspension from American League president Ban Johnson. The pitcher made up for the lost time by throwing both halves of a pair of September doubleheaders, earning splits in each. He finished the season with 26 wins and led the league with 39 complete games and 382 innings pitched.

There was constant friction between McGraw and Johnson, and the manager solved the problem by jumping from Baltimore in the American League to the National League New York Giants and taking McGinnity and a number of other Orioles with him. In 1903, his first year with the Giants, McGinnity won 31 games and set National League records with 48 games started and 434 innings pitched. In 1904, he won a career-best 35 games, 14 of them consecutively, and posted a 1.61 earned run average. But there would be no World Series because of the continuing feud between McGraw and Johnson.

When the Giants returned to the World Series in 1905, Christy Mathewson threw three shutouts. The other victory completing the championship was another shutout, this one by McGinnity.

By 1908, McGinnity was not only pitching but also coaching third base for the Giants. He was there when Fred Merkle neglected to touch second base and the Cubs' Johnny Evers called for the ball to record a force-out.

That was McGinnity's last year in the Major Leagues. He was not done with baseball, though, and spent another 14 years in the minors with five 20-win seasons and one 30-win season. He pitched his last game in 1925 at the age of 54 and died four years later.

PITTSBURGH PIRATES

Fred Clarke

At a time of frequent change and instability in baseball, Fred Clarke was a constant in Pittsburgh, managing the Pirates for 16 seasons and playing left field for most of those years. He piloted the team to 1,422 wins, four pennants, 14 straight first-division finishes, and a .565 winning percentage. All remain franchise records. He also had 180 wins as manager at Louisville before the team merged with Pittsburgh, pushing his career total to 1,602.

Clarke also was a productive player, first with Louisville and later with Pittsburgh. The tipoff to how good he could be came in his first Major League game in 1894 when he went five for five. That was after he staged what might be perceived as a wildcat strike, refusing to dress for the game until he received the $100 he had been promised by his new team. When Colonels owner Barney Dreyfuss coughed up the cash, Clarke agreed to play and delivered four singles and a triple. And when Dreyfuss took the Colonels to merge with Pittsburgh, he had the great good sense to bring Clarke along.

The five hits in his first game were the first of 2,672 career hits for Clarke, who batted .312 for his career and hit over .300 11 times. He also had 226 triples and 506 stolen bases, often batting in front of Honus Wagner and setting the table for the Pirates' best hitter. Clarke led the league in doubles and slugging percentage in 1903 while leading the Pittsburgh Pirates to the National

League championship and an appearance in baseball's first World Series. Pretty good for a guy who got into baseball by answering a help wanted ad. The Hastings team of the Nebraska State League was shopping for players, and Clarke thought it might be a good opportunity. So, at age 19, he was hired. Three years later, he was in Louisville, negotiating with Dreyfuss.

The owner must have been impressed because, three years after Clarke arrived in Louisville, Dreyfuss named the youngster manager of the team. Now faced with the double responsibility of managing and playing, Clarke responded with his best season, batting .390, second best in the league behind Wee Willie Keeler's .424. The team did not fare as well, finishing next to last. But Dreyfuss stuck with Clarke, and armed with a fistful of young, talented players, Louisville merged with Pittsburgh in 1900, and the new team, managed by Clarke, finished second. A year later, the Pirates were champions, and Clarke was the toast of the town.

The next year, Clarke's team tore through the league, going 103–36 to win the pennant by 27½ games. The Pirates were armed with a nucleus of outstanding players led by Wagner, who led the league in runs (105), doubles (30), runs batted in (91), and stolen bases (42). Clarke flourished as well, batting .316 and scoring 103 runs.

The Pirates won a third straight pennant in 1903 when Clarke and Wagner gave the team a devastating 1–2 punch. Clarke led the league in doubles (32) and slugging percentage (.532) while batting .351, four points behind Wagner. Delighted with his team, Dreyfuss arranged a World Series against the American League champion Boston Red Stockings. But with their pitching staff staggered by injuries and illness, the Pirates team lost the best-of-nine series in eight games.

Pittsburgh stayed in the chase for the next few years when the Last Chicago Cubs Dynasty fell into place. Clarke's Pirates interrupted the dynasty in 1909, reaching another World Series, this time against Detroit. Even though he was approaching 40, Clarke led all outfielders in fielding percentage that season and hit two home runs in the Series as the Pirates defeated the Tigers.

Honus Wagner

Perhaps the greatest player of baseball's Deadball Era was Pittsburgh's remarkable Honus Wagner. He was a member of the Hall of Fame's inaugural class in 1936 after a brilliant 21-year career in which he compiled a career batting average of .328, led the league in hitting eight times, and batted over .300 in 15 consecutive seasons. When he retired, Wagner held Major League records for games (2,792), runs (1,736), hits (3,415), and total bases (4,862). He also held National League records for doubles (640) and triples (252) and drove in 1,732 runs, second only to Cap Anson's 1,879. He also stole 723 bases, leading the league in that department five times, and played every position except catcher. He was, then, the era's most complete and dynamic performer.

He hardly looked the part. Wagner was bow-legged and barrel-chested, a body that belied his skills on the diamond. He grew up working in the coal mines of western Pennsylvania and followed his older brother, Albert, into baseball. At age 21, he started out with Steubenville of the Inter-State League in 1895, eventually playing for four other teams in three leagues that year. Wherever he played, though, the young Wagner showed that he could hit. He never batted less than .365 that year and caught the eye of Ed Barrow, later general manager of the New York Yankees. Barrow guided Wagner to Patterson, New Jersey, of the Atlantic League and then recommended him to Barney Dreyfuss, owner of the Louisville franchise.

Wagner broke in with Dreyfuss's team on July 19, 1897, and batted .338 in 61 games, mostly as a center fielder. Three years later, he was in Pittsburgh when Dreyfuss's Louisville team was merged with the Pirates. Wagner was an immediate star in the National League, winning his first batting title in 1900 when he led the league in triples, doubles, and slugging percentage. It was also the first of three straight National League pennants for the Pirates.

This was an era of players jumping from team to team and even league to league. In 1901, the Chicago White Stockings of the American League offered Wagner $20,000 to leave Pittsburgh. But he turned them down, preferring to stay with Dreyfuss's team, which was emerging as a powerhouse.

Pittsburgh played Boston in baseball's first World Series in 1903, but Wagner struggled mightily, batting just .222. He was terribly distressed by his performance and set out to make up for it. Over an eight-year stretch, he won seven batting titles and finished second once. He led the league in doubles five times, slugging and on-base percentage four times each, stolen bases three times, and RBIs and triples twice each. He was tearing up baseball.

After the 1907 season, Wagner was 33 and decided he had had enough of baseball. He announced his retirement from the game and sat out spring training, a baseball ritual he never enjoyed. Dreyfuss refused to accept Wagner's departure, and $10,000 later, his star was back with the Pirates and put together his greatest season. He batted .354 with 10 home runs and 109 RBIs, missing the Triple Crown by just two homers. He led the league in hits (201), doubles (39), triples (19), and stolen bases (53). He hardly looked ready for retirement.

Wagner's hitting tear continued in 1909 when the Pirates interrupted the Last Chicago Cubs Dynasty by winning 110 games, the most in franchise history, and the National League pennant. Wagner won another batting title, hitting .339, and also led in slugging (.489), on-base percentage (.420), doubles (39), and RBIs (100). The World Series against Detroit was billed as a showdown between Wagner and Ty Cobb, and the Pirates star won easily, batting .333 to Cobb's .231, driving in six runs to five for Cobb and stealing six bases to Cobb's two. The Pirates won the Series in seven games.

Wagner played eight more years, winning another batting title in 1911 and leading the league with 102 RBIs in 1912. He ranks among the all-time top 15 in four categories: hits (3,451), doubles (640), stolen bases (723), and at-bats (10,430).

Deacon Phillippe

When the World Series began in 1903, it matched Pittsburgh, the National League champion, against Boston, which won the American League title. There was, however, one problem for the Pirates. Their pitching staff was in disrepair, stripped by injury and illness. And that explains why Deacon Phillippe pitched five complete games and won three, all three that the Pirates won.

Phillippe started his Major League career with the Louisville Colonels in 1899 and pitched a no-hitter in his seventh game. He went 21–17 that year and threw 321 innings. A year later, he was one of a fistful of players that owner Barney Dreyfuss moved to Pittsburgh and Phillippe responded with four straight 20-win seasons.

At a time when baseball was crowded with a population of rowdy and unruly characters, Phillippe was a straight shooter. He was low key; he didn't drink, smoke, or chew tobacco; and he kept a civil tongue, which explains why Charles Phillippe picked up the nickname Deacon.

He was a control specialist who averaged just 1.25 walks per nine innings, the best ratio in the history of baseball after the 60-foot, 6-inch distance from the mound to home plate was introduced. And when Jesse Tannehill and Jack Chesbro jumped to the American League in 1903, he became the ace of the Pirates staff, responding with a 25–9 record. He also became the Pirates' best option for the World Series when 20-game winner Sam Leever came down with a sore arm and Ed Doheny, who had won 16 games, suffered a nervous breakdown.

Phillippe started the Series opener and beat Boston and Cy Young with a six-hitter. Two days later, he threw a four-hitter for another win, and after a day of travel and a rainout gave him two days' rest, he won Game Four of the Series, giving the Pirates a 3–1 lead in the best-of-nine championship.

But he was arm weary by then, and the Red Stockings took advantage. Phillippe pitched two more complete games, but Boston beat him both times to win the Series. His five complete games remain a World Series record that almost certainly will never be broken. Pirates owner Barney Dreyfuss was so impressed with Phillippe's efforts that he gave the pitcher 10 shares of stock in the club.

The workload took its toll on Phillippe, and he struggled to a 10–10 record the next year before recovering to win 20 games for the sixth time in 1905. But arm woes continued to trouble him, and when the Pirates interrupted the Last Chicago Cubs Dynasty by winning 110 games in 1909, Phillippe worked largely out of the bullpen and compiled a 14–2 record. He also hit an inside-the-park grand-slam home run, no small accomplishment for a pitcher whose lifetime batting average was .189.

In 1969, he was voted the best right-handed pitcher in Pittsburgh history.

12

WHERE THEY PLAYED—THEN AND NOW

Sometimes, it seems as if the Chicago Cubs have played baseball in Wrigley Field forever. The cozy little ballpark nestled in a neighborhood on the North Side of the city had a baseball history long before Harry Caray began a tradition of leaning out of his broadcast perch during the seventh-inning stretch to lead the crowd in a rendition of "Take Me Out to the Ballgame," and long before they began flying pennants from the center-field flagpole to signal the result of the game—white with a blue *W* for a Cubs victory and blue with a white *L* for a loss.

This cathedral of baseball celebrated its 100th anniversary in 2014 and then underwent some extensive renovations. It was sort of like an elderly dowager, putting on lipstick and makeup, and looking young all over again. The fact of the matter, though, is that Chicago's National League team moved around town several times before the current home of the Cubs was built in 1914 to house another team.

The town's ballpark odyssey began in 1871 after Mrs. O'Leary's legendary cow either did or didn't kick over a bucket— accounts differ on the event's origin—setting fire to the city. At the time, Chicago's National Association club, then known as the White Stockings, had laid claim to a dumping ground on the shores of Lake Michigan, but the Union Base-Ball Grounds burned to the ground in the fire. The team completed the 1871 season on the road and did not return to its own park until 1874 when it settled at the 23rd Street Grounds.

It was while the National Association White Stockings were playing at 23rd Street that William Hulbert, owner of the team, became disgusted with Boston's dominance in the standings and the loose lifestyle of the players and decided to launch a new league for his team. The National League opened for business in 1876 with Hulbert's Chicago entry playing at the 23rd Street Grounds. That was a temporary landing spot but home to some historic firsts in baseball. On May 2, second baseman Ross Barnes, lured by Hulbert from Boston to Chicago along with pitcher Albert Spalding and catcher Deacon White, hit the first National League home run, the only one he hit all season. That same year, Chicago outfielder Bob Addy earned a niche in the history of the game by being the first player to slide into a base. The team was a powerhouse, winning the first National League pennant with a 52–14 record. Spalding won 47 games, and Barnes batted .429 and led the league in hits, doubles, triples, and walks. The next year, though, Chicago plunged to a fifth-place finish. Spalding was done as a dominant pitcher, and White, unencumbered by the reserve clause that did not appear until sometime later, jumped back to Boston. Meanwhile, the White Stockings became the only National League team to go through an entire season without hitting a home run.

A year later, Hulbert moved his team to Lake Front Park I, where it played in rather Spartan conditions with a beat-up infield surface for five seasons. The condition of the field led the White Stockings to commit over 300 errors every year they played in Lake Front Park I, with a high of 389 in 1880. It was a quirky facility with the right-field fence less than 200 feet away and ground rules calling any ball hit over the wall a double. The park was also in need of some refurbishing, and Hulbert made a $10,000 investment to move his team into a more modern park that was a showplace for baseball. Lake Front II was the largest facility in the game with a capacity of 10,000. That included 18 rows of private boxes equipped with curtains and armchairs, fore-runners of today's luxury suites. There was, however, the matter of the same old odd dimensions. The left-field fence was just 180 feet from home plate. Right field measured 196 feet. In 1883, a ball hit over the left-field fence was a double. The next year, it was a home run. In 1883, the White Stockings hit 277 doubles but just 13 home runs. The next year, with the new ground rules in place, they hit more than 100 fewer doubles and 142 home runs. Those measurements turned out to be a great benefit for Ned Williamson, who set an National League record with 50 doubles in 1883 and then hit 27 home runs the next year. In 1884, Williamson also became the first player to hit three home runs in a game. But because of the frequent change in ground rules, 19th-century baseball statistics must be viewed rather warily.

By 1885, the team moved on again to the first West Side Park, sometimes referred to as the West Side Grounds, and this dou-ble-decked structure, circled by a bicycle track, remained its home for 23 seasons, throughout the team's dynasty in the first decade of the 20th century. Construction was complicated, forc-ing the team to spend the first five weeks of the season on the road. That was no problem for manager Cap Anson's powerhouse ball club. They came home with an 18–6 record and opened their new home on June 6 by beating the St. Louis Maroons. Chicago was on its way to an 87–25 season and the league championship. They repeated the first-place finish the next year, going 90–34, giving Chicago five titles in seven years. Lean times were ahead, however, and the team did not finish first again until 1906, the start of the Last Chicago Cubs Dynasty.

In 1891, the team split its home schedule between two parks: West Side Park on Mondays, Wednesdays, and Fridays and South Side Park II on Tuesdays, Thursdays, and Saturdays. That arrangement ended after two years, and by 1894, the team had moved into the new West Side Grounds, located a few blocks from the first West Side Park but closer to the World's Columbian Exposition, a sort of world's fair that could help the baseball team's attendance. But the new home was not without drama. On August 5, during a game against Cincinnati, the ballpark caught fire. Forty fans were injured in the melee to evacuate the park, but it could have been worse. Several players rescued fans by pulling down a wire fence, providing an escape route. The ball yard was quickly repaired with the same combustible wood that had burned Chicago ballparks before, and the team went about its business.

West Side Grounds had more modern distances in the outfield. It was 340 feet down the left-field line and 316 feet to the fence in right field. Center field measured a spacious 560 feet, and on July 13, 1896, Philadelphia's Ed Delehanty took advantage of the ballpark's wide open outfield spaces and became the second player in Major League history to hit four home runs in a game, all of them inside the park. A year later, with the team struggling to a 59–73 record in Cap Anson's last year as manager, Chicago enjoyed one remarkable game. Playing against Louisville on June 29, the team set a Major League record by scoring 36 runs. They had 32 hits, six of them by shortstop Barry McCormick, five by pitcher Nixey Callahan and four apiece by center fielder Bill Lange and second baseman Jim Connor. They were helped along by nine Louisville errors. The offensive outburst came after Chicago had managed just two runs in its previous two games. The 36 runs remained the Major League record well into the 21st century.

By the time it scored the 36 runs in one game, the team was called the Colts. Later, with Anson gone, the nickname became the Orphans. It was not until 1902 that they became the Cubs, at a time when Chicago was assembling a team of stars, one that would dominate the National League in the first decade of the 20th century.

Chicago became a two-team town when the American League was granted Major League status in 1901, and the White Sox opened for business on the South Side, creating a dandy rivalry for the hearts and minds of the city's population. It also led to a major disappointment for the National League champion Cubs in 1906 when the underdog White Sox won the only all-Chicago World Series.

By 1913, a third team had squeezed into the city. Baseball was thriving, and its success intrigued some more investors who created the new Federal League, which attracted some familiar names. Cy Young would manage Cleveland. Deacon Phillippe piloted Pittsburgh. Even Chicago stalwarts Mordecai Brown and Joe Tinker signed on, Brown as pitcher-manager for St. Louis, Tinker to manage the ChiFeds. A year later, there was a continued exodus of familiar Major League names headed for the Federal League. Eddie Plank and Chief Bender left the Philadelphia Athletics. Former Cubs ace Ed Reulbach came over from Brooklyn, and Hooks Wiltse moved from the New York Giants. Future Hall of Famers Edd Roush and Bill McKechnie began their pro careers in the new league.

Charles Weeghman, a dining-car magnate, had failed in an attempt to purchase the St. Louis Cardinals in 1911 but surfaced again as the owner of the Chicago Whales of the new Federal League. He invested $250,000 to build a handsome new concrete and steel ballpark for his team on the northwest side of Chicago at the intersection of Clark and Addison streets. Construction took just six weeks. The league had a short shelf life. Weeghman's ballpark, however, lasted much longer.

Staggered by meager attendance, the Federal League folded after the 1915 season, but Weeghman wasn't going anywhere. He put together a syndicate including chewing-gum magnate William Wrigley Jr. to purchase the Cubs and moved them out of the shabby West Side Grounds and into his fancy new facility with a capacity of 14,000. The place was named after the owner— Weeghman Park.

By then, the Cubs had fallen on hard times on the playing field. After Frank Chance left, the managerial hot seat belonged to Cubs legend Johnny Evers for one year; Hank O'Day, the umpire in the middle of the Fred Merkle boner play in 1908, for one year; Hall of Fame catcher Roger Bresnahan for one year; and Evers's double-play partner Joe Tinker for one year. None of them had much success. The struggles continued in the team's fancy new home. The Cubs finished in fifth place in 1916 but were a hit at the gate, nearly doubling their attendance from the year before. The ballpark at the corner of Clark and Addison was becoming a baseball centerpiece.

The next year, one of the most remarkable games in baseball history took place at the home of the Cubs. On May 2, 1917, Chicago's Jim "Hippo" Vaughn and Fred Toney of Cincinnati matched nine innings of hitless baseball. The Reds pushed across a run in the top of the 10th and then Toney completed his half of the double no-hitter. The pitching excellence must have been contagious because, before the week was over, teammates Ernie Koob and Bob Groom of the St. Louis Browns threw their own no-hitters on consecutive days against the White Sox.

Weeghman Park went through another name change in 1919, rechristened Cubs Park. In 1921, Wrigley headed a group of Chicago businessmen who bought the club, and by 1926, the ballpark had another new name. Now, the home of the Cubs would be called Wrigley Field, a name that turned out to have more staying power than any that preceded it.

By then, the ballpark's seating had been expanded to 20,000, and a year later, it was up to 30,000. The next year, a double deck was added with the new seating that stretched from the right-field corner to left field, increasing capacity to 40,000. Baseball was flourishing in the little ballpark on the North Side of Chicago. And when the Cubs were away, Wrigley hosted all manner of events, including football, boxing, rodeos, and even concerts. They even played an ice hockey game there in 2009, part of the National Hockey League's Winter Classic series. The place became a Chicago landmark.

On the field, however, the Cubs were struggling, going 18 years with just one pennant. The lone title came in 1918, with America's attention diverted by its entry into World War I. The Cubs, perhaps flushed by their sudden success, made a deal with the crosstown White Sox to host the first three World Series games against Boston in roomier Comiskey Park. Attendance was anemic, however, reducing income for the players, who were already annoyed by a new rule that distributed Series shares to all teams finishing in the first division. Before Game Four in Boston, the angry players on both teams threatened to strike. With a plea to their patriotism, baseball officials talked them into playing, and the Sox prevailed in six games, depriving Wrigley Field of its first World Series.

The 1918 Series was also a one-man show for Babe Ruth, then pitching for the Red Sox. He throttled the Cubs, winning both his starts, although his Series shutout string ended at 29⅔ innings. He also had a two-run triple in Game Four, a hint of the kind of slugger he would become in the years ahead.

A year later, the Black Sox World Series scandal rocked baseball, and it was a Cubs stockholder, A. D. Lasker, who recommended federal judge Kenesaw Mountain Landis be hired as commissioner to administer the sport.

It was another 11 years before Wrigley Field had another chance at hosting World Series baseball.

Meanwhile, professional football was in its infancy, hardly considered a major sport. George Halas, who had played baseball, football, and basketball at the University of Illinois, helped the Illini to the Big Ten championship and was Most Valuable Player of the 1919 Rose Bowl. Even though he played big league baseball briefly for the New York Yankees, his future was on the gridiron. In 1920, he helped organize the National Football League, and a year later, shopping for a place for the local team to play, he met with William Wrigley, by then boss of the Cubs and proprietor of the ballpark at the corner of Clark and Addison. With the park standing idle after the baseball season ended, it was a perfect marriage, and until 1970, the Chicago Bears called the home of the Cubs their home as well. Originally, Halas's team was known as the Decatur Staleys, but they changed the name to Bears as a tribute to their landlords. In 1925, with the NFL just getting started, Halas made a preemptive strike by signing University of Illinois star running back Red Grange to a $100,000 contract and taking his Bears on a 16-game barnstorming trip to show off his new prize player. A crowd of 36,000 packed Wrigley Field for Grange's first game as a pro on November 26, with the Bears and Chicago Cardinals playing to a 0–0 tie. Grange gained just 36 yards but did much better after that. The irony of the team's move to its new home was that in its first year at the park, Halas's team won the league championship, an achievement that proved exceedingly difficult for the landlord Cubs to duplicate.

By 1926, Cubs Park had been renamed Wrigley Field, and the owner began upgrading his facility—eventually investing $2.3 million—adding an iconic marquee in front of the building, constructing an upper level to increase seating and adding bleachers, providing a home to the Cubs' most ardent fans. A year later, the investment began paying off when the Cubs became the first National League team to draw over one million fans in a season.

Three years later, the Cubs were back on top of the National League, winning the pennant by 10½ games with a lineup packed with Hall of Famers such as Rogers Hornsby, Gabby Hartnett, Kiki Cuyler, and Hack Wilson. Wrigley Field drew 1.5 million fans and played host to its first World Series against Philadelphia. The Cubs lost the first two games at home but then won Game Three and charged out to an 8–0 lead in Game Four, seeming well on their way to tying the Series. But Connie Mack's Athletics rallied, scoring 10 runs to win the game and taking a commanding 3–1 lead in the Series. The A's then won Game Five and the world championship. That disappointment did not diminish the enthusiasm of the Cubs fans. On June 27, 1930, a ladies day promotion against the Brooklyn Dodgers squeezed a crowd of 51,556 into the ballpark. It was the largest crowd in Wrigley Field history.

Wrigley was impressed with a young sportswriter who had covered the 1919 Black Sox scandal under the byline "Bill Bailey." The writer was William Veeck, and Wrigley hired him away from journalism to work in the Cubs front office. The deal included Veeck's four-year-old son, William Jr., who proved to have a major impact on a number of baseball franchises as well as the home of the Cubs.

As he grew up, the younger Veeck worked for the team during summer vacation from school. When William Wrigley died in 1932, operation of the Cubs passed to his son, Philip Wrigley. That was the same year that the Cubs returned to the World Series, only to be swept by the New York Yankees. Old pal Babe Ruth, now a slugger instead of a pitcher, provided an exclamation point with his "Called Shot" home run, an event that would be debated by baseball scholars into the 21st century.

By 1933, Arch Ward, sports editor of the *Chicago Tribune*, had convinced the proprietors of baseball to hold an exhibition game, inviting the best players in the sport to play for charity. The All-Star Game would become an annual event, a moment in the baseball summer for the game to take a deep breath and celebrate its best players. The first game was played across town from Wrigley Field, at Comiskey Park, home of the American League White Sox. Wrigley Field did not get to host an All-Star Game until 1947, when fans voted for the starting lineups for the first time. But Wrigley had its own memorable moment in 1933 when the football tenant Bears beat the New York Giants there to win the first National Football League championship.

Two years later, the Cubs were back in the World Series, using a remarkable 21-game winning streak to win the National League pennant. After winning Game One against Detroit, Chicago dropped the next three. The Cubs won Game Five to send the Series back to Detroit. Game Six was tied 3–3 when Stan Hack led off the ninth inning with a triple. But he was stranded there, and the Tigers won the game and the Series in the bottom of the ninth. It was another disappointment for the Cubs and Wrigley Field.

In 1938, the Cubs returned to the Series again, this time on a dramatic home run by Gabby Hartnett as darkness closed in on Wrigley Field. Waiting for them again were the Yankees, and again the Cubs were swept. Wrigley would remain without a World Series winner.

Meanwhile, young Veeck had become a handyman around the team, first as an office assistant but later with expanded duties. His outgoing personality made a perfect ambassador for the team. He would roam the ballpark, visiting fans and trying to make their ballpark experience more enjoyable. Part of that effort, Phil Wrigley decided, was to continue updating the ballpark, making it a cozier place to watch baseball. He promoted the home of the

Cubs as "Beautiful Wrigley Field," and in 1937, the assignment to make it beautiful went to Veeck.

Veeck remembered the ivy-covered fences he admired at minor league Perry Stadium in Indianapolis and decided to replicate the look at Wrigley Field. There were other changes—a handsome new three-story scoreboard, new bleachers, wider seats, and concession stands designed to make Wrigley Field more fan friendly. And there would be greenery: 200 Boston ivy plants decorating the outfield walls, planted by young Veeck himself. Originally, the plan was to plant trees, but Chicago's harsh weather vetoed that idea. In a rush to provide the greenery Wrigley wanted, Veeck planted 350 Japanese bittersweet and supplemented it with the ivy that took over the walls and became a trademark of "Beautiful Wrigley Field." A ball that stuck in the ivy—and many did—was a ground rule double. If it bounced out of the ivy, it was a live ball. Veeck moved on to other baseball adventures with the Cleveland Indians (where he introduced Larry Doby as the American League's first black player), the St. Louis Browns (where he sent a midget, Eddie Gaedel, up as a pinch hitter), and the Chicago White Sox (where he had a scoreboard that celebrated home runs with fireworks). The ivy thrived on the Wrigley walls he left behind. Charles Weeghman would be proud.

All around baseball, teams were moving toward night games. President Franklin Delano Roosevelt threw a switch in Washington to illuminate Cincinnati's Crosley Field for the first night game on May 24, 1935. It was the first of eight night games at Cincinnati that season, and even though the Reds struggled to a 68–85 record, home attendance increased by 117 percent. Night baseball was a hit.

The Cubs were having nothing of the trend though—at least not publicly. But P. K. Wrigley understood that his ballpark would one day have to embrace the change, and in 1941, the Cubs owner stored tons of steel and electrical equipment under the bleachers, intending one day to install lights in Wrigley Field. On December 8, 1941, the day after the Japanese bombed Pearl Harbor, Wrigley donated all of the material to the war effort. Wrigley Field would remain an outpost—eventually the last one—for day baseball.

The Cubs returned to the World Series once more—their fifth and final time since the Last Chicago Cubs Dynasty—in 1945, and this time it seemed things would fall their way against Detroit. They got a shutout by Hank Borowy in the opener and another one by Claude Passau in Game Three. But Game Four provided a turning point in the history of the team. Local tavern keeper Billy Sianis brought his goat to the game, a decision that did not sit well with Wrigley Field management. Sianis and his goat were summarily escorted out of the park. The tavern keeper did not go quietly, angrily cursing the Cubs in perpetuity. Never again, Sianis declared, would the home team find World Series success at Wrigley Field. The Tigers won the 1945 Series in seven games. The Cubs took the Curse of the Billy Goat one step further. Never again have they even played a World Series game at Wrigley Field.

When Charles Weeghman built this ballpark, he certainly never thought about the wind patterns off nearby Lake Michigan. Over the years, however, they have become a major part of the Wrigley Field experience. When the wind is blowing out, simple fly balls often become home runs. And when it is blowing in, long balls headed for the bleachers often wind up in the gloves of outfielders.

On August 25, 1922, when Wrigley was still called Cubs Park, the Phillies were in town and got into an offensive slugfest with the home team. The two second-division teams combined for 49 runs, 51 hits, 23 walks, and 25 men left on base. The Cubs scored 10 runs in the second inning and 14 in the fourth to build a 25–6 lead. Two Phillies pitchers, Jimmy Ring and Lefty Weinert, absorbed the abuse. Cliff Heathcote reached base seven times with three singles, two doubles, and two walks. Marty Callaghan batted three times in the 14-run fourth, getting two hits before striking out. Then the home crowd held its breath as Philadelphia came roaring back with eight runs in the eighth and six in the ninth to close the gap to 26–23. The Phillies had the bases loaded in the ninth inning when the final out was recorded. The game remains the highest score in Major League baseball history.

Fifty-seven years later, on May 17, 1979, the Cubs and Phillies got into another Wrigley slugfest. Hall of Famer Mike Schmidt hit a 10th-inning home run to give Philadelphia a 23–22 victory in a game the Cubs had trailed 21–9 before rallying to force extra innings. The homer was Schmidt's second in a game in which Dave Kingman hit three homers for the Cubs. Kingman is also credited with Wrigley's longest homer, a shot estimated at 550 feet in 1976, when he was with the New York Mets.

Conversely, Ken Holtzman's first no-hitter, on August 19, 1969, against Atlanta, included a seventh-inning blast by Henry Aaron that had home run written all over it until it got caught up in one of Wrigley's trademark wind gusts and left fielder Billy Williams was able to leap and catch it. Without the wind, Aaron's career home run total would have been 756 instead of 755.

Modern baseball required modern stadiums, and Chicago recognized that trend. In 1964, P. K. Wrigley proposed a new domed stadium for the city, a venue that would be shared by the Cubs, White Sox, and Bears. The $34 million stadium would seat between 55,000 and 60,000 fans and replace elderly Soldier Field. The Bears agreed to the idea, but the White Sox passed, leaving the Cubs still playing in the last stadium without lights.

This became a major issue with baseball moving its glamorous events like the All-Star Game, playoffs, and World Series games to prime time to accommodate its television partners. In 1984, baseball's new commissioner, Peter Ueberroth, informed the

Cubs that without lights any postseason games would not be played at Wrigley Field.

Four years later, despite the opposition from traditionalists who loved day games at Wrigley Field, lights were lowered into place by helicopters and installed at the venerable ballpark. The first scheduled night game on August 8, 1988, was rained out after three innings, perhaps a message from a higher authority that Wrigley's day-game tradition should have been preserved.

Wrigley's history included some landmark events. Besides the Hippo Vaughn–Fred Toney double no-hitter in 1917, Babe Ruth's "Called Shot" home run in 1932, and Gabby Hartnett's "homer in the gloamin'" in 1938, there were Ernie Banks's 500th career home run in 1970; Pete Rose's 4,191st hit to tie Ty Cobb's record in 1985; Kerry Wood's 20-strikeout game in 1998; Sammy Sosa's 60th home runs in 1998, 1999, and 2001; Greg Maddux's 3,000th career strikeout in 2005; and Tom Glavine's 300th victory in 2007.

However, progress demanded change, and current owner Tom Ricketts, who met his wife in the bleachers at Wrigley Field, committed to a $575 million upgrade of the grand old ballpark and its environs. The changes included electronic signs and scoreboards, all the bells and whistles of modern ballparks. Sadly, however, the updated bleachers, long a centerpiece of the old ballpark, were not ready for the start of the 2015 season. But the improvements guaranteed that Wrigley would be a baseball showplace for years to come.

NOTES

1. PRELUDE TO A DYNASTY

1. Peter Golenbock, *Wrigleyville* (New York: St. Martin's, 1996), 15.

2. David Pietrusza, Matthew Silverman, and Michael Gershman, eds., *Baseball: The Biographical Encyclopedia* (Kingston, NY: Total/Sports Illustrated, 2000), 1217.

3. "1883 Chicago White Stockings Roster," accessed September 18, 2015, Baseball Almanac, http://www.baseball-almanac.com/.

4. Golenbock, *Wrigleyville*, 95.

5. Harold Kaese, *The Boston Braves 1871–1953* (New York: Putnam, 1954), 186.

6. Ibid.

2. ASSEMBLING THE DYNASTY

1. Kaese, *Boston Braves*, 55.

2. Rob Neyer and Eddie Epstein, *Baseball Dynasties* (New York: Norton, 2000), 38–39.

3. Gerald Astor, ed., *The Baseball Hall of Fame 50th Anniversary Book* (New York: Prentice Hall, 1988), 47.

4. National Baseball Hall of Fame and Museum, *The Hall : A Celebration of Baseball's Greats*, official 75th anniversary book (New York: Little, Brown, 2014), 265.

5. Lawrence Ritter, *The Glory of Their Times* (New York: Harper Perennial, 1992), 121.

6. "Mordecai Brown Stats," Baseball Almanac, accessed September 19, 2015, http://www.baseball-almanac.com/.

7. "1907 World Series," Baseball Almanac, accessed September 19, 2015, http://www.baseball-almanac.com/.

8. Astor, *Baseball Hall of Fame*, 47.

9. Fred Lieb, *Baseball as I Have Known It* (New York: Putnam, 1977), 188.

10. Golenbock, *Wrigleyville*, 155.

3. WHO'S HITLESS NOW?

1. "John McGraw Quotes," Baseball Almanac, accessed September 19, 2015, http://www.baseball-almanac.com/.

2. Ed Sherman, "The 1906 World Series Featuring the Cubs and Sox," *Chicago Tribune*, accessed September 19, 2015, http://www.chicagotribune.com/.

3. Jim Margalus, "Fielder Jones: From the Hall of Fame Library Player Files," SB Nation, November 22, 2011, http://www.southsidesox.com/.

4. Golenbock, *Wrigleyville*, 124.

5. "George Rohe," Baseball Library, accessed September 20, 2015, http://www.baseballlibrary.com/.

4. REVENGE

1. Sherman, "The 1906 World Series."

2. "John McGraw Quotes," Baseball Almanac.

3. Ritter, *Glory of Their Times*, 59.

4. "Ty Cobb Quotes," Baseball Almanac, accessed September 20, 2015, http://www.baseball-almanac.com/.

5. "Ty Cobb," *Wikipedia*, last updated September 19, 2015, https://en.wikipedia.org/.

6. Ibid.

7. Gil Bogen, *Johnny Kling : A Baseball Biography* (Jefferson, NC: McFarland, 2006), 103.

8. Lee Lowenfish, *Branch Rickey , Baseball's Ferocious Gentleman* (Lincoln: University of Nebraska Press, 2007), 469.

5. ONCE MORE WITH FEELING

1. Ray Robinson, *Matty, an American Hero* (New York: Oxford University Press, 1993), 101.

2. Golenbock, *Wrigleyville*, 145.

6. 104 WINS ARE NOT ENOUGH

1. Ritter, *Glory of Their Times*, 59.

2. "Ty Cobb," Baseball Library, accessed September 20, 2015, http://www.baseballlibrary.com/.

7. AND THEN . . .

1. John Thorn, "Babe Ruth's Autobiography, as Written in 1920; Section III," *Our Game* (blog), April 8, 2015, http://our-game.mlblogs.com/.

2. Lowenfish, *Branch Rickey*, 194.

3. "Gabby Hartnett," *Wikipedia*, last updated September 18, 2015, https://en.wikipedia.org/.

4. Astor, *Baseball Hall of Fame*, 169.

5. David Fulk and Dan Riley, eds., *The Cubs Reader* (Boston: Houghton Mifflin, 1991), 34.

8. CURSES, CATS, AND OTHER CALAMITIES

1. "Billy Sianis," *Wikipedia*, last updated May 3, 2015, https://en.wikipedia.org/.

2. Jeff Merron, "No Masking Horror of Friday the 13th," ESPN Page 2, March 6, 2012, http://espn.go.com/.

3. Jerome Holtzman, "Was the Cubs 'College of Coaches' a Complete Failure? To a Degree . . . ," *Chicago Tribune*, December 21, 1986.

10. FACES OF THE FRANCHISE—OLD AND NEW

1. Pietrusza, Silverman, and Gershman, *Baseball*, 31.

2. "Ernie Banks Quotes," Baseball Almanac, accessed September 22, 2015, http://www.baseball-almanac.com/.

3. Craig Muder, "Inside Pitch," National Baseball Clubhouse Hall of Fame, October 23, 1974, http://community.baseballhall.org/.

11. THE OTHER GUYS

1. "Connie Mack Quotes," Baseball Almanac, accessed September 23, 2015, http://www.baseball-almanac.com/.

2. "Christy Mathewson Quotes," Baseball Almanac, accessed September 23, 2015, http://www.baseball-almanac.com/.

BIBLIOGRAPHY

BOOKS

Ahrens, Art. *Tinker to Evers to Chance*. Charleston, SC: Arcadia, 2007.

Alvarez, Mark, ed. *SABR Baseball Research Journal* 22 (1993).

Astor, Gerald, ed. *The Baseball Hall of Fame 50th Anniversary Book*. New York: Prentice Hall, 1988.

Bogen, Gil. *Johnny Kling: A Baseball Biography*. Jefferson, NC: McFarland, 2006.

Carr, Jason, and Dani Holmes, eds. *Chicago Cubs Media Guide*. Chicago: Chicago Cubs Baseball Club, 2010.

Coberly, Rich. *The No-Hit Hall of Fame: No-Hitters of the 20th Century*. Newport Beach, CA: Triple Play Publications, 1985.

Cohen, Richard M., and David S. Neft, eds. *The World Series Complete Play-By-Play*. New York: Macmillan, 1986.

Dewey, Donald, and Nicolas Acocella. *Total Ballclubs*. Toronto: Sport Media Publishing, 2005.

Dickey, Glenn. *The History of National League Baseball*. Briarcliff Manor, NY: Stein and Day, 1979.

Enright, Jim. *Baseball's Great Teams: Chicago Cubs*. New York: Macmillan, 1975.

Fulk, David, and Dan Riley, eds. *The Cubs Reader*. Boston: Houghton Mifflin, 1991.

Golenbock, Peter. *Wrigleyville*. New York: St. Martin's, 1996.

Grove, Samuel. "Chicago." In *Encyclopedia Americana*, 427–28. New York: Americana Corp., 1973.

Kaese, Harold. *The Boston Braves 1871–1953*. New York: Putnam, 1954.

Lewis, Oscar. "San Francisco." In *Encyclopedia Americana*, 204. New York: Americana Corp., 1973.

Lieb, Fred. *Baseball as I Have Known It*. New York: Putnam, 1977.

Lowenfish, Lee. *Branch Rickey, Baseball's Ferocious Gentleman*. Lincoln: University of Nebraska Press, 2007.

Lowry, Philip J. *Green Cathedrals*. Reading, MA: Addison-Wesley, 1992.

Mack, Connie. *My 66 Years in the Big Leagues*. Mineola, NY: Dover, 2009.

Mead, William B. *Two Spectacular Seasons*. New York: Macmillan, 1990.

National Baseball Hall of Fame and Museum. *The Hall: A Celebration of Baseball's Greats*. Official 75th anniversary book. New York: Little, Brown, 2014.

National Baseball Hall of Fame and Museum Yearbook. Lynn, MA: H. O. Zinman, 2015.

Neyer, Rob, and Eddie Epstein. *Baseball Dynasties*. New York: Norton, 2000.

Okkonen, Marc. *The Federal League of 1914–1915*. Garrett Park, MD: Society for American Baseball Research, 1989.

Okrent, Daniel, and Harris Lewine, eds. *The Ultimate Baseball Book*. Boston: Houghton Mifflin, 1984.

Palmer, Pete, and Gary Gillette, eds. *The Baseball Encyclopedia*. New York: Barnes and Noble Books, 2004.

Patten, William, and J. Walter McSpadden, eds. *The Book of Baseball: The National Game from the Earliest Days to the Present Season*. New York: Collier, 1911.

Pietrusza, David, Matthew Silverman, and Michael Gershman, eds. *Baseball: The Biographical Encyclopedia*. Kingston, NY: Total/Sports Illustrated, 2000.

Reichler, Joseph L. *The Baseball Trade Register*. New York: Macmillan, 1984.

Ritter, Lawrence. *The Glory of Their Times*. New York: Harper Perennial, 1992.

Robinson, Ray. *Matty, an American Hero*. New York: Oxford University Press, 1993.

Shannon, Bill, and George Kalinsky. *The Ballparks*. New York: Hawthorn, 1975.

Snyder, John. *Cubs Journal*. Indianapolis: Emmis, 2005.

Society for American Baseball Research. *Deadball Stars of the National League*. Edited by Tom Simon. Washington, DC: Brassey's, 2004.

Wilbert, Warren N., and William Hageman. *The Chicago Cubs: Seasons at the Summit*. Champaign, IL: Sports Publishing, 1997.

NEWSPAPERS AND WEBSITES

Baseball Almanac, http://www.baseball-almanac.com/

Baseball Library: The Home of Baseball History, http://www.baseball library.com/

Baseball Reference, http://www.baseball-reference.com/

Chicago Tribune, http://www.chicagotribune.com/
Chicago Tribune archives
Cubs.com, http://www.chicagocubs.com/
ESPN, http://www.espn.com/
Legacy.com, http://www.legacy.com/
National Baseball Clubhouse Hall of Fame, http://community.baseballhall.org/
National Baseball Hall of Fame and Museum, http://www.baseballhall.org/
Pastime Post, http://www.pastimepost.com/
SABR: Society for American Baseball Research, http://www.sabr.org/
Sports Business journal
Wikipedia: The Free Encyclopedia, http://www.wikipedia.org/

INDEX

ABOUT THE AUTHOR

Hal Bock was an award-winning sportswriter and columnist for 40 years at the Associated Press, where he covered the full panorama of sports events, including 30 World Series, 30 Super Bowls, and 11 Olympic Games. He also taught journalism at Long Island University and St. John's University. Bock is the author or editor of 14 books, including the narrative for *The Associated Press Pictorial History of Baseball* and, most recently, *Willard Mullin's Golden Age of Baseball Drawings*. He lives in East Williston, New York, with his wife, a retired psychologist, and their cat, a rescued stray.